THE
PASSION
TRANSLATION

THE PASSIONATE LIFE BIBLE STUDY SERIES

12-LESSON STUDY GUIDE

THE BOOK OF
PSALMS
PART TWO
The Psalms of Comfort

poetry on fire

BroadStreet
PUBLISHING

BroadStreet Publishing® Group, LLC
Savage, Minnesota, USA
BroadStreetPublishing.com

TPT: The Book of Psalms, Part 2: Psalms of Comfort: 12-Lesson Study Guide
Copyright © 2023 BroadStreet Publishing Group

9781424566280 (softcover)
9781424566297 (ebook)

Stock or custom editions of BroadStreet Publishing titles may be purchased in bulk for educational, business, ministry, fundraising, or sales promotional use. For information, please email orders@ broadstreetpublishing.com.

General editor: Brian Simmons
Managing editor: William D. Watkins
Writer: Christy Phillippe

Cover and typesetting by Garborg Design Works | Garborgdesign.com

Printed in China

23 24 25 26 27 5 4 3 2 1

Contents

From God's Heart to Yours

"God is love," says the apostle John, and "Everyone who loves is fathered by God and experiences an intimate knowledge of him" (1 John 4:7). The life of a Christ-follower is, at its core, a life of love—God's love of us, our love of him, and our love of others and ourselves because of God's love for us.

And this divine love is reliable, trustworthy, unconditional, other-centered, majestic, forgiving, redemptive, patient, kind, and more precious than anything else we can ever receive or give. It characterizes each person of the Trinity—Father, Son, and Holy Spirit—and so is as limitless as they are. They love one another with this eternal love, and they reach beyond themselves to us, created in their image with this love.

How do we know such incredible truths? Through the primary source of all else we know about the one God—his Word, the Bible. Of course, God reveals who he is through other sources as well, such as the natural world, miracles, our inner life, our relationships (especially with him), those who minister on his behalf, and those who proclaim him to us and others. But the fullest and most comprehensive revelation we have of God and from him is what he has given us in the thirty-nine books of the Hebrew Scriptures (the Old Testament) and the twenty-seven books of the Christian Scriptures (the New Testament). Together, these sixty-six books present a compelling and telling portrait of God and his dealings with us.

It is these Scriptures that *The Passionate Life Bible Study Series* is all about. Through these study guides, we—the editors and writers of this series—seek to provide you with a unique and welcoming opportunity to delve more deeply into God's precious Word, encountering there his loving heart for you and all the others he loves. God wants you to know him more deeply, to love him more devoutly, and to share his heart with others more frequently and freely. To accomplish this, we have based this study guide series on The Passion Translation of the Bible, which strives to "reintroduce the passion and fire of the Bible to the English reader. It doesn't merely convey the literal meaning of words. It expresses God's passion for people and his world by translating the original, life-changing message of God's Word for modern readers." It has been created to "kindle in you a burning desire to know the heart of God, while impacting the church for years to come."[1]

In each study guide, you will find an introduction to the Bible book it covers. There you will gain information about that Bible book's authorship, date of composition, first recipients, setting, purpose, central message, and key themes. Each lesson following the introduction will take a portion of that Bible book and walk you through it so you will learn its content better while experiencing and applying God's heart for your own life and encountering ways you can share his heart with others. Along the way, you will come across a number of features we have created that provide opportunities for more life application and growth in biblical understanding.

 ### Experience God's Heart

This feature focuses questions on personal application. It will help you live out God's Word and to bring the Bible into your world in fresh, exciting, and relevant ways.

 ### Share God's Heart

This feature will help you grow in your ability to share with other people what you learn and apply in a given lesson. It provides guidance on using the lesson to grow closer to others and to enrich your fellowship with others. It also points the way to enabling you to better listen to the stories of others so you can bridge the biblical story with their stories.

The Backstory

This feature provides ancient historical and cultural background that illuminates Bible passages and teachings. It deals with then-pertinent religious groups, communities, leaders, disputes, business trades, travel routes, customs, nations, political factions, ancient measurements and currency...in short, anything historical or cultural that will help you better understand what Scripture says and means.

Word Wealth

This feature provides definitions for and other illuminating information about key terms, names, and concepts, and how different ancient languages have influenced the biblical text. It also provides insight into the different literary forms in the Bible, such as prophecy, poetry, narrative history, parables, and letters, and how knowing the form of a text can help you better interpret and apply it. Finally, this feature highlights the most significant passages in a Bible book. You may be encouraged to memorize these verses or keep them before you in some way so you can actively hide God's Word in your heart.

Digging Deeper

This feature explains the theological significance of a text or the controversial issues that arise and mentions resources you can use to help you arrive at your own conclusions. Another way to dig deeper into the Word is by looking into the life of a biblical character or another person from church history, showing how that man or woman incarnated a biblical truth or passage. For instance, Jonathan Edwards was well known for his missions work among native American Indians and for his intellectual prowess in articulating the Christian faith, Florence Nightingale for the reforms she brought about in healthcare, Irenaeus for his fight against heresy, Billy Graham for his work in evangelism, Moses for the strength God gave him to lead the Hebrews and receive and communicate the law, and Deborah for her work as a judge in Israel. This feature introduces to you figures from the past who model what it looks like to experience God's heart and share his heart with others.

The Extra Mile

While The Passion Translation's notes are extensive, sometimes students of Scripture like to explore more on their own. In this feature, we provide you with opportunities to glean more information from a Bible dictionary, a Bible encyclopedia, a reliable Bible online tool, another ancient text, and the like. Here you will learn how you can go the extra mile on a Bible lesson. And not just in study either. Reflection, prayer, discussion, and applying a passage in new ways provide even more opportunities to go the extra mile. Here you will find questions to answer and applications to make that will require more time and energy from you—if and when you have them to give.

As you can see above, each of these features has a corresponding icon so you can quickly and easily identify them.

You will find other helps and guidance through the lessons of these study guides, including thoughtful questions, application suggestions, and spaces for you to record your own reflections, answers, and action steps. Of course, you can also write in your own journal, notebook, computer document, or other resource, but we have provided you with space for your convenience.

Also, each lesson will direct you toward the introductory material and numerous notes provided in The Passion Translation. There each Bible book contains a number of aids supplied to help you better grasp God's words and his incredible love, power, knowledge, plans, and so much more. We want you to get the most out of your Bible study, especially using it to draw you closer to the One who loves you most.

Finally, at the end of each lesson you'll find a section called "Talking It Out." This contains questions and exercises for application that you can share, answer, and apply with your spouse, a friend, a coworker, a Bible study group, or any other individuals or groups who would like to walk with you through this material. As Christians, we gather together to serve, study, worship, sing, evangelize, and a host of other activities. We grow together, not just on our own. This section will give you ample opportunities to engage others with some of the content of each lesson so you can work it out in community.

We offer all of this to support you in becoming an even more faithful and loving disciple of Jesus Christ. A disciple in the ancient world was a student of her teacher, a follower of his master. Students study, and followers follow. Jesus' disciples are to sit at his feet and listen and learn and then do what he tells them and shows them to do. We have created *The Passionate Life Bible Study Series* to help you do what a disciple of Jesus is called to do.

So go.

Read God's words.

Hear what he has to say in them and through them.

Meditate on them.

Hide them in your heart.

Display their truths in your life.

Share their truths with others.

Let them ignite Jesus' passion and light in all you say and do.

Use them to help you fulfill what Jesus called his disciples to do: "Now wherever you go, make disciples of all nations, baptizing them in the name of the Father, the Son, and the Holy Spirit. And teach them to faithfully follow all that I have commanded you. And never forget that I am with you every day, even to the completion of this age" (Matthew 28:19–20).

And through all of this, let Jesus' love nourish your heart and allow that love to overflow into your relationships with others (John 15:9–13). For it was for love that Jesus came, served, died, rose from the dead, and ascended into heaven. This love he gives us. And this love he wants us to pass along to others.

Why I Love the Book of Psalms: Comfort

Life can bring us sorrow and stress. We lose someone we love. We go through a trial that tests our faith. We are pushed into corners by those who reject us. What do you do when you don't know what to do?

I read a psalm until my heart is at rest.

I have loved the book of Psalms for over fifty years. They steady my soul when my steps falter. Their comfort brings me peace when there is nothing peaceful in my environment. I have never gone to the Psalms in my hour of need and failed to experience the comfort of God, who has offered his embrace to us through the Psalms.

The soothing words I read in the Psalms recharge and restore me. Their bright melodies turn the dark clouds into rainbows of refreshing. When I pour over the words of David, I often feel like I have found a friend, a man who understands the movements of my life. David was not afraid to display his emotions. He tasted the sting of grief and shame, he walked through dark valleys (like we do!), yet he continually returned to the comfort of God's love. I love the Psalms because they become a mirror to my soul. These mercy-filled verses encourage me to go on.

> The comfort of your love takes away my fear.
> (Psalm 23:4)

> Whenever my busy thoughts were out of control, the soothing comfort of your presence calmed me down and overwhelmed me with delight. (94:19)

> Send your kind mercy-kiss to comfort me, your
> servant, just like you promised you would. Love
> me tenderly so I can go on, for I delight in your
> life-giving truth. (119:76–77)

I love the Psalms because their truths have rescued me from despair and set my feet to dancing. Get ready to receive the greatest, heart-warming words you'll ever read. They are found in the Psalms. May the God of all comfort bring you the light of hope as you study these lyrics of love.

And may the Lord himself "turn and comfort us once again" (71:21).

Brian Simmons
General Editor

LESSON 1

Welcome to the Book of Psalms

Lord, you know everything there is to know about me.
You perceive every movement of my heart and soul,
and you understand my every thought
before it even enters my mind.
You are so intimately aware of me, Lord.
You read my heart like an open book
and you know all the words I'm about to speak before I even
start a sentence!
You know every step I will take before my journey even begins.
…Where could I go from your Spirit?
Where could I run and hide from your face?
If I go up to heaven, you're there!
If I go down to the realm of the dead, you're there too!
If I fly with wings into the shining dawn, you're there!
If I fly into the radiant sunset, you're there waiting!
Wherever I go, your hand will guide me;
your strength will empower me.
It's impossible to disappear from you
or to ask the darkness to hide me,
for your presence is everywhere,
bringing light into my night.

—Psalm 139:1–4, 7–11

A passionate relationship with God is the heart-cry of every person, but many of us don't know how to express our praise, our prayers, or our passion to God. When we face times of heartbreak, jubilation, confusion, loss, or thanksgiving, it may be difficult to find the words to share our thoughts and feelings with the Lord in prayer. The book of Psalms is a help and a comfort to all of us, for it allows us to pray and praise along with the writers as they express the deepest longings of their hearts and the most exuberant worship and thanks for God's amazing work in their lives.

The book of Psalms is a model of praise and prayer that we can follow. In fact, many believers have prayed through the Psalms, making the passages their own as they use them to speak and cry out to God and listen for his voice as he speaks to them. Psalms is a collection of different groups of prayers and songs used by the people of God for centuries, beginning in Old Testament times. The word *psalms* comes from the Greek word *psalmos*, translated from the Hebrew word *mizmor*, which means "songs" or "a poem set to notes."[2] In the centuries before Jesus was born, the Psalms helped a largely illiterate population learn and remember God's Word by setting his words to music. They also played a critical role in the community as the people came together to worship God in the temple as well as in the many synagogues.

- *Have you ever had trouble finding the words to express your thoughts and feelings to God or difficulty putting language to your heart's deepest feelings and concerns? Describe a time or two when this occurred.*

- *Did you find a way to get past this time? What did you do and learn from it?*

Authorship

The Psalms were composed by a number of people who lived in Old Testament times: David wrote seventy-three psalms; his son, King Solomon, wrote two. Other authors include Asaph, the sons of Korah, Jeduthun, Heman, Etan, and Moses. The various psalms were collected over centuries, but most were written between the time of David's reign (ca. 1000 BC) and Ezra's ministry (ca. 450 BC).

The book of Psalms that we have in our Bibles today is a collection that is divided into five sub-collections, or books, which seem to relate to the Pentateuch—the first five books of the Hebrew Bible. The Pentateuch is a book of instruction for God's people, just as the book of Psalms is a kind of instruction manual on worshiping God and going to him with our joys and sorrows.

A popular phrase some years ago provoked thought by asking, "What would Jesus do?"—enabling believers to consider different options when they faced confusion in life or had to make important decisions. As we read the book of Psalms, we could consider the question "How would David pray?" when we need help expressing our thoughts and feelings to the Lord.

- *Have you ever used one or more of the psalms in the Bible to express your feelings to God? If so, what was the result? If you have not, do you think this would help you as you engage with God in prayer? In what ways?*

Key Themes

The book of Psalms is a book of poetry, which is interpreted differently from other books in the Bible, such as a book of history (including Genesis or Exodus) or a letter of Paul. Poetry uses fluid language, including metaphors and poetic techniques that are not usually meant to be taken literally. The psalms express deep emotion and are typically meant to be read in a devotional way. Still, different psalms had different uses for the original worshipers, and they have different uses for us today. Many psalms are hymns of praise through which we join with the writer in acknowledging the greatness and the majesty of our God. Some are psalms of lament through which we express our sorrow for sin, a request for God to intervene in our life circumstances, a desire to see God's enemies punished, or a plea to God for help. Other psalms include songs of thanksgiving, wisdom psalms meant to teach or instruct God's people, or songs sung within God's community as they gathered at the temple.

𝕟 WORD WEALTH

The Hebrew word *Selah* is found throughout the book of Psalms. Many people believe that it indicates a place to stop and think about what has just been read or spoken aloud. The translator of The Passion Translation has used the phrase "Pause in his presence" to indicate where this phrase is used in the Psalms. Here is what the translator, Brian Simmons, says about the translation of this word:

> The Hebrew word *Selah* [is] a puzzling word to translate. Most scholars believe it is a musical term for pause or rest. It is used a total of seventy-one times in the Psalms as an instruction to the music leader to pause and ponder in God's presence. An almost identical word, *Sela*, means a massive rock cliff. It is said that when *Selah* is spoken that the words are carved in stone in the throne room of the heavens.[3]

As you pause in God's presence throughout this study, consider how God also pauses to listen to you.

A Mirror into Our Souls

The book of Psalms is a beautiful, eloquent collection of patterns for prayer. Essentially, in Psalms, prayer has been married to poetry, and here, we find expression for all the emotions of life. The fourth-century church father Athanasius wrote this about the book of Psalms:

Among all the books [of the Bible], the Psalter has certainly a very special grace, a choiceness of quality well worthy to be pondered; for, besides the characteristics which it shares with others, it has this peculiar marvel of its own, that within it are represented and portrayed in all their great variety the movements of the human soul. It is like a picture, in which you see yourself portrayed, and seeing, may understand and consequently form yourself upon the pattern given. Elsewhere in the Bible you read only that the Law commands this or that to be done, you listen to the Prophets to learn about the Savior's coming, or you turn to the historical books to learn the doings of the kings and holy men; but in the Psalter, besides all these things, you learn about yourself. You find depicted in it all the movements of your soul, all its changes, its ups and downs, its failures and recoveries. Moreover, whatever your particular need or trouble, from this same book you can select a form of words to fit it, so that you do not merely hear and then pass on, but learn the way to remedy your ill.[4]

John Calvin wrote this about Psalms, calling it "an anatomy of parts of the soul":

There is not an emotion of which anyone can be conscious that is not here represented as in a mirror. Or rather, the Holy Spirit has here drawn to the life all the griefs, sorrows, fears, doubts, hopes, cares, perplexities, in short, all the distracting emotions with which the minds of men are wont to be agitated.[5]

- *What is your favorite psalm? Why?*

 EXPERIENCE GOD'S HEART

Any good relationship requires a give-and-take in communication. One person talks, and another person listens and responds. The entire Bible consists of God's Word to us. We listen to his words, learn from his teaching, and consider the lives of God's people who have gone before us. The book of Psalms adds a dimension to this that the other books of Scripture do not. In Psalms, we hear God's people using words to reach out to the Lord. Other books of the Bible contain divine encounters and some occasional prayers, but no other solely comprises prayers and praises to God as Psalms does. Consequently, through this book, we can learn how to respond to God and answer his words to us. His Word is not meant for us to simply read and then set aside; we are to answer him in prayer and in actions as we pursue a personal relationship with him that fulfills the deepest longings of our heart.

• *What deep emotions have you struggled to express to God?*

• *How do you anticipate the book of Psalms helping you with your prayer life and your worship of the Lord?*

♥ SHARE GOD'S HEART

Praising and worshiping God are meant not only to be individual efforts but also to be a community undertaking. The same is true of prayer. It surely is important to cultivate your own times of prayer and worship with the Lord, but we must also not neglect to come together for times of prayer, praise, worship, and collective petitioning for the needs of one another and those still outside of Christ.

- *How does your experience of prayer and worship differ when you are alone and when you are gathered with other believers?*

- *Is there someone in your life who is struggling with his or her relationship with God? How might the book of Psalms bring comfort to that person?*

- *Is there someone who is experiencing great joy? How could you join with him or her in thanking God for his blessings?*

Talking It Out

Since Christians grow in community, not just in solitude, here are some questions you may want to discuss with another person or in a group. Each "Talking It Out" section is designed with this purpose in mind.

1. Do you set aside certain times of the day to spend in prayer, or do you "make your life a prayer" (1 Thessalonians 5:17) as you go about your daily activities? Or perhaps both?

2. Have you gone to the Psalms before to find comfort? If so, did you find help there? Discuss your answer.

3. What answers are you hoping to find through this Bible study?

LESSON 2

Comfort in Times of Sorrow and Despair

(Psalm 88)

Additional psalms about facing sorrow and despair: 6, 42, 43

If you live long enough on this earth, you are certain to face a time of sorrow or even despair. From the smallest child who skins his knee to the older person who loses her spouse to cancer, throughout the life span of every person, pain and grief are intimate parts of the human experience.

The late Vince Havner, a popular Christian writer and evangelist, wrote about the death of his wife in one of his last published books:

> I think of a year that started out so pleasantly
> for my beloved and me. We had made
> plans for delightful months ahead together.
> Instead, I sat by her bedside and watched
> her die of an unusual disease. She expected
> to be healed, but she died. Now, all hopes of
> a happy old age together are dashed to the
> ground. I plod alone with the other half of
> my life on the other side of death. My hand
> reaches for another hand now vanished and
> I listen at night for the sound of a voice that

is still. And I am tempted a thousand times to ask, "My God, why...?"

But still, you need never ask "Why?" because Calvary covers it all. When before the throne we stand in Him complete, all the riddles that puzzle us here will fall into place and we shall know in fulfillment what we now believe in faith— that all things work together for good in His eternal purpose. No longer will we cry "My God, why?" Instead, "alas" will become "Alleluia," all question marks will be straightened into exclamation points, sorrow will change to singing, and pain will be lost in praise.[6]

Have you ever experienced what some Christians have called the "dark night of the soul"? What do you do when it appears that your life is falling apart and God seems nowhere to be found?

Psalm 88 has been labeled the "saddest psalm in the Bible," and that certainly could be true. The author of this psalm seems overcome with despair. He weeps before God "night and day" (v. 1); he feels a "heavy weight," as if he is "drowning...beneath a sea of sorrow" (v. 7). Worse, God himself seems to have turned the other way (v. 14), and the psalmist feels left "all alone with only darkness as [his] friend" (v. 18). Unlike many other psalms, this one doesn't even end on a hopeful note; it's as though the writer thinks he will never experience hope again.

Have you ever been there? Have you ever felt as if something so terrible, so significant, so utterly life-changing has occurred that you believe your hope will never return? Whether it feels like it or not, God is with you.

Let's look more closely at this psalm of comfort.

⬚ THE BACKSTORY

According to the Scriptures, the author of Psalm 88 is Heman the Ezrahite rather than King David, who wrote most of the other psalms in the Bible. This "Heman" was not a superhero with an animated television show some decades ago; far from it. The Heman who authored Psalm 88 lived thousands of years ago, likely during the reign of King David, most Bible scholars agree, and he was a worship leader in the temple of Solomon. He was, more than likely, appointed as a worship leader by King David himself, which tells us a lot about Heman's skill since the king himself was a great songwriter and worship leader. In fact, Heman was so skilled at worship that he was put in charge of training 288 other skilled musicians in the temple.

- *Read through Psalm 88. Does it seem to have been written by someone who loved the Lord or by someone who did not believe in him? Explain your answer.*

Many Bible scholars believe that Heman had some sort of serious affliction, perhaps an illness that had plagued him his entire life. Heman does write that he couldn't remember a time when he felt good or was without pain. Others postulate that he may have lost a child or other loved one, which could have prompted the writing of this psalm.

- *Using your imagination, consider what type of suffering Heman might have been experiencing to pen the words of Psalm 88. What would cause someone to pray this kind of prayer?*

- *Does this psalm strike a chord in your soul? Can you relate to Heman's grief or confusion or brokenness? If so, what happened that has led you into this time of deep hurt?*

Honest Hurt and Petition

Although the words of Psalm 88 may seem shocking in their brutal honesty, the fact is, God is never shocked—not by the words we pray and not by the feelings in our hearts. He would much prefer our honesty with him about our suffering and our gut-wrenching emotions, even our doubts, than for us to pray pious, meaningless prayers that don't reflect what our hearts are experiencing.

Heman was desperate. Whatever the circumstances were that he was facing, he was past the point of hollow, meaningless prayers. In our moments of greatest desperation, there is no time for clichés.

- *Read Psalm 88 again and consider the various problems Heman was facing. What was going wrong in each of the following areas?*

    His physical health:

    His finances:

    His emotional health:

    His relationships with other people:

His relationship with God:

• *Why do you suppose God seemed silent to Heman?*

 DIGGING DEEPER

Heman is not the only character in the Bible to have struggled with overwhelming problems and feelings of isolation from the Lord. In fact, many of the great heroes of the faith experienced these emotions. One of the most familiar is Job, a man who likely lived before Moses during the time of the patriarchs (Abraham, Isaac, and Jacob).[7] Job faced extreme upheaval in his life to the point that his wife and his friends even urged him, in a quasi-suicide mission, to "Curse God and die" (Job 2:9 NLT).

- *Read through the first two chapters of the book of Job. List here as many problems Job faced as you can uncover:*

- *What is the worst problem you have ever faced? Like Job, did you face a health crisis? Financial troubles? The death of a loved one? Tell the story.*

• *What was your response to the problem? Was it ever resolved? If so, how?*

• *Did your faith in God help to support and guide you during that time? Why or why not?*

Many Christians look at the life of Job and believe that because he lived during the time of the Old Testament, before Jesus' redeeming work on the cross, he faced problems that we, as New Testament believers, should never have to face. However, Paul, one of the greatest missionaries in the early church and the writer of a significant portion of the New Testament, also faced more problems than, at times, he knew how to handle. At one point, he even despaired of life itself. Here's what he said in 2 Corinthians 1:8–11:

> Brothers and sisters, you need to know about the severe trials we experienced while we were in western Turkey. All of the hardships we passed through crushed us beyond our ability to endure, and we were so completely overwhelmed that we were about to give up entirely. It felt like we had a death sentence written upon our hearts, and we still feel it to this day. It has taught us to lose all faith in ourselves and to place all of our trust in the God who raises the dead. He has rescued us from terrifying encounters with death. And now we fasten our hopes on him to continue to deliver us from death yet again, as you labor together with us through prayer. Because there are so many interceding for us, our deliverance will cause even more people to give thanks to God. What a gracious gift of mercy surrounds us because of your prayers!

- *How can you justify Paul's feelings at the beginning of this passage with his belief in Jesus as the risen Son of God? (See also 2 Corinthians 11:22–29.)*

- *According to Paul, what made the difference in pulling him out of his discouragement and despair? In whom was he taught to lose faith? Where did he put all of his trust and fasten all of his hopes?*

- *How could doing the same make a difference in your own attitude toward troubling times?*

- *Do you believe it is possible to have faith and yet feel cut off from God's favor and blessing? Why or why not?*

Our Ultimate Blessing

Most Christians, when faced with difficult times, look toward the ultimate blessing that believers in Jesus will experience: eternal life with God in heaven, where there is no more sorrow, no more death, no more tears. Many believers and leaders in the church throughout history have maintained this heavenly focus. Dwight L. Moody, American evangelist and founder of Moody Bible Institute, wrote of the contrast between this life and the next: "This is the land of sin and death and tears, but up yonder... is unceasing joy."[8]

- *Have you ever looked to the promise of heaven during tough times? How did it help you—or not help you—to get through the challenges you faced?*

DIGGING DEEPER

Scattered throughout the Old Testament, starting as far back as Genesis and Job, the Hebrews found indications that they would live beyond the grave and that their after-death life would be with God (e.g., see Job 19:25–27; cf. Genesis 22:2–5 with Hebrews 11:17–19[9]; Psalm 16:10–11; Ecclesiastes 12:5–7; Daniel 12:2–3, 13). Jesus, a Jew by birth, argued as much when he reached back into the book of Exodus and concluded that the God who identified himself in Moses's day as the God of Abraham, Isaac, and Jacob (three men who had long ago passed away) was the God of the living, not of the dead (Mark 12:26–27; Exodus 3:13–16). God's covenant was not with the dead but with the living, which included those individuals whose bodies were now in graves and yet were still living with God.

Many other passages in the Old Testament gave careful and thoughtful readers confidence that God's people would have life on the other side of death,[10] but nowhere could one find anything about everlasting life as clear and developed as what would come in the New Testament writings. The teaching, death, resurrection, and ascension of Jesus provided a welcome, fresh, and brighter light than Old Testament revelation gave. And through the Spirit's inspiration, some of the apostles, especially Paul, illuminated the future life with revelation that the ancient Hebrews never had (e.g., see Luke 16:19–26; John 5:25–29; 11:25–26; Romans 8:11; 1 Corinthians 15; Revelation 20–21).

So what did Heman believe about what God would do for him, not just in this life but also in the life hereafter? For the most part, Hebrews such as Heman were looking for God's covenant promises to be fulfilled in their earthly lifetimes. All the miracles the children of Israel witnessed during their exodus from Egypt took place on earth. They literally saw the Red Sea part, manna fall from heaven, and a physical rock spew forth water for them to drink. And when they worshiped God, they praised him for providing for their daily needs. Their primary orientation was fixed on this world, with hints of an afterlife and even of another world yet to come.

- *What New Testament beliefs do we in the modern age of the church take for granted that Old Testament believers in Yahweh might not have had? List as many as you can think of.*

Heman would have had an Old Testament perspective. As a worship leader in King David's temple, he would have been aware of the praise songs the children of Israel had known, the song Miriam sang when the Red Sea closed over their Egyptian enemies, sealing their deliverance from slavery. He might have known of his king's words in Psalm 23, which praised the Lord for his shepherding care that provided nourishment and safety. But in Psalm 88, Heman felt far from nourished and far from safe.

- *Recall the earthly needs Heman expresses or implies in Psalm 88. How might a knowledge of New Testament revelation have helped to change Heman's perspective?*

⦿ EXPERIENCE GOD'S HEART

Despite the pessimism and pain Heman felt in Psalm 88, he followed several principles from which we can learn about our own experience with God.

First, despite his immense pain and grief, Heman continued to hold on to God and remain before him in prayer. He didn't cry out to others; he cried out to the one who could help.

Second, Heman was honest about his feelings. Brutally so, almost. He realized what we also need to remember: God already knows what we are experiencing and how we are feeling in the deepest recesses of our hearts. Rather than try to hide those feelings from him, we would do well to bring them before him as we pray.

Third, Heman was willing to wait. Psalm 88 seems to indicate that Heman was not going anywhere until he had an answer from the Lord. He was insistent that God come through for him. He refused to give up.

- *What challenges are you facing right now that might (or might not) rival Heman's?*

- *How honest with God have you been about those challenges, including how they make you feel?*

- *Go ahead and write a brutally honest prayer to the Lord right now. Pour out your heart without censoring your feelings. Remember, he already knows how you feel.*

 SHARE GOD'S HEART

When was the last time you went to church and asked a friend or acquaintance, "How are you?" Chances are, the reply was, "Doing great," or "Couldn't be better." Isn't it strange that church is one of the many places where we tend to put on a "happy face," dressing our best and wearing our biggest smiles, no matter what we are actually going through?

- *Why do you think so many people have a hard time sharing at church the challenges they are facing and the hurt and pain they are experiencing?*

- *How does Jesus want his church to respond to hurting people?*

- *Is there someone you know who is facing a difficult time?*
  Perhaps they are going through a divorce, recently lost a
  job, or received a bad health report. Reach out to them and
  offer a listening ear this week with no judgment or advice.
  Just offer to let them talk and then be present for them.

Talking It Out

1. In recent decades, many church circles have propagated the
   "prosperity gospel," or the "name it and claim it" doctrine.
   In essence, people who adhere to this doctrine believe
   that you can have abundant blessings here on earth by
   "claiming" them—including financial riches, perfect health,
   and wonderful relationships with family and friends. What
   do you think about these beliefs? What might someone who
   believed in the prosperity gospel have said to Heman? How
   might Heman have felt upon receiving their advice?

2. Should a Christian ever feel depressed or hopeless? Should we, as believers, ever visit a mental health professional for depression or anxiety or take psychotropic medication? Explain your answer.

3. Heman seemed to blame God for some of his problems in Psalm 88. Is it possible to go too far in accusing the Lord of wrongdoing, even when you are being brutally honest in your prayers? Why or why not? How is it possible to honestly wrestle with your experiences while still maintaining your love of and trust in God?

LESSON 3

Comfort When You Feel Abandoned and Alone

(Psalms 31 and 41)

Additional psalms about feeling abandoned and alone: 23, 130

One all-time favorite holiday movie is *Home Alone*, which tells the story of a large, boisterous family who plans to travel to Europe for the Christmas holiday. The youngest sibling, Kevin McCallister, is annoyed with his family before the trip begins, and the night before their departure, he even announces to his mother that he wishes he never had a family. In a bizarre set of circumstances, as the family is rushing out the door to make their flight the next morning, Kevin is left behind, and when he later wakes up in an empty house, he believes his wish has actually come true: he has made his family disappear!

At first, the experience is great for Kevin. He eats whatever he wants (lots of ice cream!) and watches whatever he wants on TV—no one to bother him, no one to annoy him. But after a series of events in which he manages to take care of himself while fending off a pair of bungling burglars, Kevin realizes he misses his family after all. Being abandoned and alone isn't the thrill he had thought it would be.

The truth is that God made us to need one another. And when someone—especially a trusted friend or family member—abandons or betrays us or when we feel lonely, as if no one in the world cares, it's a painful experience. Mother Teresa once said,

"The biggest disease today is not leprosy or tuberculosis, but rather the feeling of being unwanted, uncared for and deserted by everybody."[11]

THE BACKSTORY

King David, the writer of Psalms 31 and 42, understood what it felt like to be alone, afraid, abandoned by those he thought were his friends. Long before he became the king, he found himself hunted and on the run from King Saul, for whom he had killed the giant Goliath, for whom he had played the harp to soothe King Saul's distress. But Saul was jealous of David's growing popularity, and when that jealousy turned into a murderous rage, David resorted to hiding out in caves to preserve his own life.

Much later, many years after David had become king, his own son Absalom mounted a campaign against him. Absalom sought to become king himself, and he plotted against his own father to overthrow David and gain the crown for himself. Even Ahithophel, David's own wisest and most trusted advisor, abandoned the king and, in a traitorous move, threw his support behind Absalom's campaign.

Most Bible scholars believe that Psalm 31 was written during one of these two incidents in David's life and that Psalm 41 was likely written during Absalom's attempt to overthrow David and take the kingdom from him. In each of these incidents in David's life, he faced a stinging betrayal by those he had trusted. And in the case of Absalom, the betrayal came from his own flesh and blood—his son.

- *Read 1 Samuel 23 and 2 Samuel 15–18. What feelings might David have experienced during these challenging situations?*

- *Has a close friend or family member ever betrayed or abandoned you? What feelings did you experience?*

Take a look at King David's words in Psalm 41:9–10:

> Even my ally, my friend, has turned against me.
> He was one I totally trusted with my life,
> sharing supper with him,
> and now he shows me nothing but betrayal and
> treachery…
> So Lord, please don't desert me when I need you!
> Give me grace and get me back on my feet
> so I can triumph over them all.

• *At the time someone betrayed or abandoned you, how were your emotions similar to (or different from) what David experienced?*

• *What did David ask of the Lord?*

- *Have you ever asked the Lord for the same thing? What was the result?*

Our Back-and-Forth Emotions

First, stop and read through Psalm 31.

Did you notice the different emotions David experienced? At first, he was filled with trust that God would rescue him from his troubles, but by verse 9, he was deep in depression and sorrow that his enemies had betrayed him—as well as his "friends and neighbors" (v. 11). Then, in desperation, by verse 14 he was determined again to trust only in the Lord, and he does so throughout the rest of the psalm.

Sometimes it's easy to forget that the heroes of our Bible—including King David—were human beings, just like we are, with emotions that wavered between loneliness and fear and confidence and doubt. Fortunately for David, his faith and trust in God secured his commitment to the Lord and gave him the courage to move forward even in the face of emotional pain and betrayal.

- *How easy is it for you to succumb to negative emotions when fear and loneliness creep into your heart?*

- *What did David do in Psalm 31:14 to renew his hope?*

- *How many reminders of God's goodness can you find in Psalm 31?*

- *How can reminding yourself of the goodness of God and his presence with you help you renew your own hope in the face of abandonment and loneliness?*

WORD WEALTH

Even in David's darkest moment, he knew the one who held his future: "My life, my every moment, my destiny—it's all in your hands" (v. 15).

- *Psalm 31:15 has been a beloved verse for many believers throughout Christian history. Write out this verse in your own words in the space below and consider memorizing it to remind yourself of God's presence and plan for you, especially during times of trouble.*

All Kinds of Trouble

David almost certainly wrote Psalm 41 during the rebellion of Absalom, perhaps around the same time as he wrote Psalm 31. In each of these psalms, David faced trouble in many different areas of his life. Just as each of us has experienced, the saying is often true: "When it rains, it pours." When something goes wrong in one area of our lives, other things are apt to go wrong as well.

Sometimes this is a coincidence, but it is true that for most of us, many areas of our lives are so interconnected that when one thing goes wrong, it can cause calamity in other areas too. When you are going through work or relationship stress, it can affect your physical health, or if you are facing a serious illness that results in medical bills and lost wages, your finances can also go haywire.

In both Psalms 31 and 41, David was experiencing an intense and lonely time of suffering. He was experiencing afflictions in every area of his life, and those around him, even friends and neighbors, despised him for it.

- *Why do you think human beings tend to flock toward those who are doing well but will reject or avoid people who seem to have "too many problems"?*

- *Have you ever experienced this? What did you do?*

 DIGGING DEEPER

First Kings 19 tells the story of God's prophet Elijah and how his victory over the prophets of Baal caused the evil queen Jezebel to seek him in order to murder him.

- *Read this chapter in 1 Kings and write out the feelings Elijah might have been experiencing.*

- *Elijah was a member of the Israelite people, living after the time of King David, and he likely knew the words of Psalm 31. Which verses in this psalm might have comforted him during this time?*

Letting Go of the Grudge

In Psalm 41, David was facing a grave illness, and most scholars believe it was during this time that either his son Absalom or another of David's enemies sensed weakness in the king and organized a strike against the kingdom, hoping to take over the throne. Whatever the illness was, the physical suffering that resulted from it was not nearly as bad as the emotional suffering caused by the betrayal of David's son and trusted advisor, Ahithophel.

- *Read 2 Samuel 11:3 and 23:34. Although Ahithophel was a wise counselor to King David, the fact remains that he was Bathsheba's grandfather, who likely still held a grudge against the king for how David had treated his granddaughter and her first husband, Uriah. According to 2 Samuel 11, what had David done that Ahithophel might have had trouble forgiving?*

- *Why is holding grudges so toxic to our relationships with others? Our relationship with God? Our own physical health?*

- *Is there anyone in your life against whom you still hold a grudge even if the air has supposedly been cleared? Could anyone be holding a grudge against you? What could you do to mend this relationship?*

- *After the betrayal of his trusted friends, David himself could have held a grudge. Read Psalm 41:9–13 and record what David did instead.*

- *If you need to do so, write a prayer below, handing over to the Lord all of your hurt feelings, even your desire for revenge against those who have betrayed or abandoned you.*

🦁 EXPERIENCE GOD'S HEART

When we are feeling alone, whether it is because someone has betrayed or abandoned us or because we are simply in a lonely time of our lives, it helps to remember that even Jesus, the Son of God, experienced feelings of loneliness while he was here on the earth. He knows how we feel—and if we call out to him, he will never leave us or forsake us (Hebrews 13:5).

Even as David was writing the words of Psalms 31 and 41, centuries before Jesus was born, he was foreshadowing the experiences of our Savior and Lord. Psalm 41:9 was actually quoted by Jesus at the Last Supper when one of his closest friends and disciples, Judas Iscariot, was about to betray him. Jesus said:

> "I don't refer to all of you when I tell you these things [his teachings at the Last Supper], for I know the ones I've chosen—to fulfill the Scripture that says, 'The one who shared supper with me treacherously betrays me.' I am telling you

this now, before it happens, so that when the prophecy comes to pass you will be convinced that I AM."...Then Jesus was moved deeply in his spirit. Looking at his disciples, he announced, "I tell you the truth—one of you is about to betray me."... The dearly loved disciple leaned into Jesus' chest and whispered, "Master, who is it?"

"The one I give this piece of bread to after I've dipped it in the bowl," Jesus replied. Then he dipped the piece of bread into the bowl and handed it to Judas Iscariot, the son of Simon...Jesus looked at Judas and said, "What you are planning to do, go do it now." None of those around the table realized what was happening. Some thought that Judas, their trusted treasurer, was being told to go buy what was needed for the Passover celebration, or perhaps to go give something to the poor. So Judas left quickly and went out into the dark night to betray Jesus. (John 13:18–30)

- *Reread Psalm 41:9 and consider what took place between Jesus and Judas Iscariot in the Gospel account. How might Jesus' emotions at the Last Supper have been similar to those of David's in Psalm 41?*

Despite the pain of betrayal by a close human friend, nothing could compare to what Jesus soon was to face on the cross. As Jesus took our sins upon himself, the Father, from whom Jesus had never been separated in all of eternity, turned his back on his Son. Jesus felt the full wrath of abandonment by God—but he did it so that those who accept his sacrifice and make him Lord of their lives would never have to feel that ultimate rejection. And when Jesus had finished paying the price for our sins, he uttered his final words on the cross.

> For three hours, beginning at noon, a sudden and unexpected darkness came over the earth. And at three o'clock Jesus shouted with a mighty voice in Aramaic, "Eli, Eli, lema sabachthani?"—that is, "My God, My God, why have you deserted me?"...Jesus passionately cried out, took his last breath, and gave up his spirit. (Matthew 27:45–46, 50)

- *Reread Psalm 31:5 and compare it with Jesus' experience on the cross. Jesus was abandoned by God so that you don't have to be, and then he entrusted his Spirit to the Father when he died—for you. Does knowing you will never be abandoned by God help with the sting of betrayal and loneliness you experience due to the actions of other people? Why or why not?*

- *American Christian writer and speaker Bill Gothard once said: "Loneliness becomes our friend that forces us to enjoy the friendship of God as much as you would the friendship of others."[12] How could time spent alone or away from the distractions of others allow you to draw closer to God?*

- *What specific steps can you take to make alone time with God a regular practice in your life?*

♥ SHARE GOD'S HEART

In our modern age of political strife, social division, and technology that leaves us more isolated from each other than ever, lonely people are all around us.[13] George Gallup, founder of the polling agency, who talked to countless people during his long career, observed: "I think we are a very lonely populace; we are cut apart from each other."[14] In some ways, abandonment and loneliness are the human condition—the result of living in a sinful, broken world. How amazing it is, then, to have a God who really sees us, who feels deeply for us, and who has acted sacrificially on our behalf! The pastor and theologian F. B. Meyer wrote: "Loneliness is an opportunity for Jesus to make Himself known."[15] It is also an opportunity for us to make Jesus known to others.

- *Who in your world needs a friend today? How will you reach out to that person this week with the love and presence of Christ?*

Talking It Out

1. Why is it that people tend to feel the most alone during times of suffering?

2. God has intended for his church, the "family of God," to be a guard against loneliness and isolation, but in many cases, people still feel alone, even among other believers. Why do you suppose this is true? What can be done to alleviate this problem?

3. In Psalm 31, David uses the Hebrew word *hesed* in verses 7, 16, and 21 to describe the love and mercy of the Lord. One definition of *hesed* describes it as a "Never-Stopping, Never Giving Up, Unbreaking, Always and Forever Love."[16] How can an authentic experience with God's *hesed* help to alleviate the loneliness we sometimes experience in this world?

LESSON 4

Comfort in Times of Fear and Anxiety

(Psalm 25)

Additional psalms about fear and anxiety: 40, 91, 102, 145

When Franklin D. Roosevelt first spoke the now-famous words, "The only thing we have to fear is fear itself," he was referring to the most pressing problem facing the United States: the Japanese aggression and Nazi atrocities that were pulling America into World War II. But those words hold true across the years and in many different situations. Fear is not a new problem for the human race. From the time Adam and Eve sinned in the garden of Eden and hid from the presence of God, fear and anxiety have been parts of the human condition.

The psalmist King David faced many times of uncertainty that led to fear, stress, and anxiety, including being chased by King Saul, who wanted to murder him; family and relationship issues; the burdens and cares of leading a kingdom; desperation and disease; the death of an infant son; and betrayal by some of his closest friends. How did David deal with this level of stress and anxiety? The first verse of Psalm 25 gives us the answer: "Always I will lift up my soul into your presence, YAHWEH."

Let's take a look at the rest of this psalm and learn how we, too, can soothe our fear and anxiety in the presence of the Lord.

THE BACKSTORY

Not only was David the king of Israel, but he was also an amazing musician, and he wrote many worship songs to be sung by the Lord's people that were later used in temple worship. Many of these songs have been preserved in the book of Psalms, and one of them is Psalm 25. Turn to that portion of Scripture now and read through it.

Did you notice how David presents requests to God but also praises him for helping him through various fearful situations? In verse 2, David asks God to not allow his enemies to defeat him (dealing with the fear of physical harm and the disgrace of defeat). In verse 4, he asks the Lord for direction and wisdom to know which way to go (which, ultimately, addresses the fear of the future). In verses 6–7, David asks for grace and forgiveness of sin (addressing the fear of failure or of sinning against God). Later in the psalm (verse 13), David affirms his desire for "prosperity and favor" (which concerns the fear of lack or of unmet needs), and in verses 15–17, he pours out his heart to the Lord, asking for mercy and freedom from loneliness, troubles, grief, misery, and "problems [that] seem to be going from bad to worse."

- *Can you relate to David's prayer in any of these areas of human need? If so, which ones?*

- *Which of these fears do you most struggle with now? Is it the fear of physical harm? The fear of defeat or disgrace? A fear of the future? A fear of failure? Of displeasing God in some way? What about a fear of material lack, needs not being met, the death of a loved one, or any number of other problems or troubles?*

- *How can the prayer of Psalm 25 help you to bring these fears before the Lord?*

Two Ways to Handle Fear

Dr. Paul Tournier, a well-known Christian psychiatrist, observed the following about fear:

> Fear creates what it fears. Fear of war impels a country to take the very measures which unleash war. The fear of losing the love of a loved one provokes us to just that lack of frankness which undermines love. The skier falls as soon as he begins to be afraid of falling. Fear of failing in an examination takes away the candidate's peace of mind and makes success more difficult.[17]

• *Have you seen this principle played out in your own life or in the life of someone you know? Tell the story.*

Many scholars consider Job to be the first book of the Bible ever written.[18] Job was a man who loved God and who had become extremely prosperous, with livestock, wealth, and many children. However, during a very short period of time, he lost everything—even his health. His wealth was gone, his children were dead, and he was covered in boils from head to toe. The situation was so bad that his wife urged him to "curse God and die" (Job 2:9 NIV) to put himself out of his misery. Amid these tremendous tragedies and his immense suffering, Job uttered the following words: "What I feared has come upon me; what I dreaded has happened to me" (3:25 NIV).

- *What do Job's words indicate about his faith in God before tragedy struck?*

- *When you survey human history—even from the time of Job—what conclusions do you come to when considering this principle of "fear creating what it fears"?*

Fortunately, we can take another response when we are experiencing anxiety or fear—of anything. That response is to turn to God and seek safety in him. David prayed this in Psalm 25:5: "Escort me into your truth; take me by the hand and teach me. For you are the God of my salvation; I have wrapped my heart into yours all day long!" The Passion Translation notes this about the last statement in this verse, which is usually translated as "I will wait upon the LORD":

> The Hebrew word most commonly translated as *wait* (wait upon the Lord) is *qavah*, which also means "to tie together by twisting" or "to entwine" or "to wrap tightly." This is a beautiful concept of waiting upon God, not passively, but entwining our hearts with him and his purposes.[19]

- *In which response to fear do you usually engage? Do you allow your fears to dominate your heart to the point of actually causing what you fear to come to pass? Or do you ask the Lord to take you by the hand and wrap your heart into his, allowing your fears to melt away in his presence?*

- *Why do you think David referred to the Lord as "the God of my salvation" in this context (Psalm 25:5)? What does salvation have to do with dealing with fear? How might releasing your fears and placing your trust in the Lord relate to the fact that he is also the one who brings salvation to us?*

𝕳 WORD WEALTH

As the worship leader of the Israelite people, David wrote many songs to be sung in worship. To help the people remember the words to these songs, David wrote some of his psalms in acrostic form, including Psalm 25. This means that each of the twenty-two verses of Psalm 25 corresponds to one of the twenty-two letters in the Hebrew alphabet. By writing this psalm using this common memorization technique, David's intention was that the people would take these words to heart and sing this song even as they left times of community worship and went about their daily lives.

- *Which of the twenty-two verses of this psalm most speaks to your heart? Write it out below.*

- *Consider memorizing this verse this week, perhaps even setting it to a familiar tune to assist you in meditating on these words of comfort in the days to come.*

 EXPERIENCE GOD'S HEART

Despite all the troubles David was experiencing and the fears that nagged at his heart, in Psalm 25 he poured out his heart to God and renewed his confidence that God was there for him, that the Lord cared about him and would see him through.

- *Reread verses 8 through 15 of Psalm 25. What allowed King David to regain his confidence in God, confidence that helped to soothe his fears?*

Many people mistake God's will for a place or a set of circumstances that they are desperately hoping will manifest in their lives. "If only…" plagues their thoughts: *If only God would give me that perfect spouse, that perfect job, that perfect place to live. If only I could find his perfect will for my life.* But the bottom line is that God's will is not a place, a situation, a house, or a job. It is a Person. When we submit our own will to him, he will always lead us on the perfect path—the path that leads us to him. God's will is always, at its core, a relationship with him. He is not a mechanical compass we consult whenever we feel lost or need direction or are afraid of what is happening in our lives. He is the Creator of the universe who wants a relationship with you. And when you put that relationship first, he will direct you, protect you, and care for your every need, leaving no need for fear in your life.

- *What would it require for you to set aside your "if onlys" and follow God's will for your life? Where do you think it would lead you?*

- *What fears would ease in your life if you were in the center of God's will?*

🌀 SHARE GOD'S HEART

When you face fearful situations with courage and trust in the Lord, others will notice—especially your close friends and family members who know the situations you are facing and can see up close how you are handling the anxiety. Consider how Ruth Bell Graham, wife of evangelist Billy Graham and daughter of medical missionary Dr. L. Nelson Bell, reacted to childhood experiences on the mission field in China that would have terrified any other young child in her situation.

Dr. L. Nelson Bell was serving as a medical missionary when the Japanese invaded China, and his family was at great risk. It was November 1938, and Sutsien, his neighbor station a few miles away, had fallen. Rumors of missionary casualties were rampant. On Christmas Day, Nelson wrote to his mother in America:

This past Thursday it was my time to lead foreign prayer meeting, and I talked about the place of physical fear in the life of the Christian. Last week it dawned on me that our Lord, tempted in all points the same as we are, yet without sin, hungered, thirsted, was tired, became angry, and gave every evidence of His humanity, but He was never fearful. Fear, therefore, must come from lack of faith—sin. Just as we never become sinless, so we never entirely lose fear, but it surely is His will for His children to live with peace in their hearts, trusting in Him and His promises.

Years later, his daughter, Ruth Bell Graham, said this in describing her growing-up years in China:

I can never recall going to sleep at night without hearing gunshots in the countryside around the house...I remember one tremendous fire over in the city. We went up to the third-story attic window where we could see it and hear the explosions. We thought the city was being invaded. The whole skyline was lit up...I think the greatest tribute to Mother's courage is that we children never sensed fear and we ourselves never had any fear. Now this is bound to reflect your parents. If they had been nervous, we would have been nervous.[20]

- *Is there someone in your life who sees your reactions to the stresses and anxieties of life, perhaps a child, family member, spouse, or close friend? Are you living out your faith and confidence in God in front of them—in both good times and bad? If not, how could you start? If so, share with them today the Source of your confidence and how he protects and steadies your heart during fearful circumstances.*

Talking It Out

1. David's practice was to find renewed strength in the Lord during times of trouble (see 1 Samuel 30:6). One way in which he did this was to write psalms and prayers to God that stemmed from the situations in which he found himself. What are some practical ways you can encourage yourself in the Lord on a daily basis? Prayer? Reading God's Word? Seeking wise Christian counsel about the issues in your life?

2. In Psalm 25:10, the word *covenant* is used—the first mention of a covenant with God in the book of Psalms. In The Passion Translation, Psalm 25 is filled with references pointing toward a covenant David had with the Lord. Which phrases do you see in which David calls upon God to keep his covenant promises? What are David's responsibilities in this covenant?

3. How can reminding ourselves of God's covenant promises to us in Christ be the greatest antidote we have against fear? (If you are unsure what this new covenant is and what Jesus Christ has to do with it, read through the New Testament book of Hebrews. You'll find most of what you need to know there.[21])

LESSON 5

Comfort during Conflict

(Psalm 55)

Additional psalms about times of conflict: 120, 126, 142

When William Palmer moved into a new house, he and his new neighbor got along just fine. They would smile broadly and wave when they saw each other in the driveway. There was no fence between their yards, and it appeared they would never need one.

The problems began when William's children began stepping in dog droppings in their yard, though they themselves didn't own a dog. The neighbor had two poodles, and William was sure they were the culprits, so one day he brought up the delicate subject. The neighbor denied that the poodles were the problem, and before long the two neighbors descended into a messy spiral of antagonism. Droppings were thrown from lot to lot. Angry words were exchanged. Signs were posted.

Eventually, the dogs disappeared, but the damage had been done.

In William's mind, the conflict reached its low point when another issue surfaced. One day he received a note from his hostile neighbor suggesting that the dead elm tree that stood squarely on the lot line between them should be cut down. William didn't like the idea of splitting the costs involved and ignored the letter. A few months later, he and his wife suddenly heard the sound of a chain saw outside. They looked out their window and watched a dead elm on their lot line as it was sawn vertically down the middle, leaving half of a grotesque dead elm standing on his property.

He left it standing for a few years as a conversation piece, then finally cut it down.[22]

What a price we pay for hostility! This tree sawn in half vertically, standing on the property line between two antagonistic neighbors, is a symbol of the pettiness, craziness, and desolation that so often accompany unresolved conflict.

Conflict—it is a normal part of life in this broken world. Most of us try to avoid it as much as possible, but the reality is that you *will* experience conflict—sometimes *serious* conflict—with other people throughout your life.

In Romans 12:18, the apostle Paul gives the following instruction: "If it is possible, as far as it depends on you, live at peace with everyone" (NIV). The Passion Translation says it this way: "Do your best to live as everybody's friend."

The question isn't, *Will I be able to escape conflict with all other people?* Of course you won't! The real question is, *How can I, a person who trusts in Jesus Christ and desires to live like him, deal with the conflict I experience in a way that honors God?*

King David went through times of extreme conflict—not just with enemies of the kingdom but also with people he trusted and loved, those who were closest to him. As we have seen in our study of previous psalms, his closest and wisest advisor, Ahithophel, betrayed David when the counselor to the king defected and joined the campaign of Absalom, David's son, who was leading a rebellion, hoping to murder his father and seize the throne. It was against the backdrop of this double betrayal—that of David's son and his closest friend—that David wrote Psalm 55. Let's take a look at it to see how he handled these intense conflicts and still remained a man after God's own heart (1 Samuel 13:14).

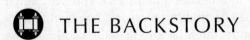 THE BACKSTORY

If, as many biblical scholars believe, the background to this psalm is the betrayal of King David by his son Absalom and his closest friend and advisor, Ahithophel, then David was not completely innocent in the conflict.

- *Read the account of David and Bathsheba in 2 Samuel 11. Also read through 2 Samuel 12, which tells of the prophet Nathan's confrontation of David's sin and the consequences it would bring. Briefly summarize the story.*

- *What was the punishment the Lord decreed as a result of David's sin? Do you think the punishment was too harsh? Too lenient? Explain your answer.*

- *What was the core reason for the family problems—*
  including the rebellion of his son—that David experienced?

In a previous lesson, we noted that Ahithophel was actually the grandfather of Bathsheba, and he had likely held a grudge against the king for some time due to David's treatment of Uriah and his granddaughter.

- *How might you have felt about King David if you were*
  Ahithophel?

- *Do you believe David's past treatment of Bathsheba influenced Ahithophel's defection to Absalom's camp? Why or why not?*

- *Is conflict ever truly one-sided? Explain your answer.*

A Heartfelt Cry

In Psalm 55, David pours out his heart to God, sharing the heartbreak, the despair, the utter desolation he feels while the conflict with his dear loved ones is ongoing. Beneath every verse of this psalm is the heart-cry of David to the Lord: "Help me!"

- *Read Psalm 55 and note how David was brutally honest with God regarding his emotions, both good and bad. Which verse rings the truest for you? Have you ever felt this way? Explain the situation.*

David's relationship troubles affect every area of his life. He is restless, with physical symptoms of stress affecting his body. He is feeling anguish, pain, turmoil, and pressure. Such consequences are not unusual. Even Jesus was in such anguish while praying in the garden of Gethsemane that he sweat drops of blood. Human beings are embodied persons who possess a soul. A person has the powers of intellect, emotion, and will. All of these aspects of a person are intricately connected, which is why feelings of anguish, fear, and dread can generate bodily suffering.

- *Describe a time when your soul was so troubled that it affected you physically. What were the symptoms you experienced in your body? How did they eventually resolve?*

God prefers his people to pray honest prayers that share with him the nitty-gritty details of our lives rather than holier-than-thou, pious-sounding prayers that lack personal transparency. Paul E. Miller, author and executive director of seeJesus Ministry, has stated: "Prayer is a moment of incarnation—God with us. God involved in the details of my life."[23]

- *David had no problem sharing every last detail of his life with the Lord. What about you? How much of the daily ins and outs of your life do you share with God?*

- *In what ways could you become more honest and open with God in your prayer life?*

The Answer to Conflict

Looking outward for a means of escape or a human way to resolve our conflicts isn't nearly as important as what David did in Psalm 55: look to God for help. Even Jesus, the very Son of God in human flesh, directly confronted conflict when he encountered the religious leaders of his day who were putting unnecessary burdens on God's people. Even with as much good as he did, Jesus was still betrayed by one of his closest friends—Judas Iscariot—who later committed suicide when he realized what he had done (Matthew 27:3–5). (Interestingly, Ahithophel also committed suicide—read 2 Samuel 17:23—as David again points us forward to Christ's future betrayal hundreds of years later.)

- *Where do you turn for comfort when a friend betrays you?*

- *What is the most recent conflict you have experienced? Has it been resolved? If so, how did God intervene to restore the relationship? If not, ask for his help now, especially to see what part you might have played in the division and what you should do to make things right.*

There is no group of people that should have a better grasp of how to maintain healthy relationships, resolve conflicts, and live in peace with one another than the followers of Jesus. Yet the believers who make up the church are not perfect. People are people—even those who are striving to become more like Christ. The New Testament church leader James wrote to one group of believers: "What is the cause of your conflicts and quarrels with each other? Doesn't the battle begin inside of you as you fight to have your own way and fulfill your own desires?" (James 4:1). This verse implies that conflict existed among God's people then—and still does today.

Our Christian fellowship, especially as believers through whom God is working, is still fellowship with fellow imperfect human beings, sinners just as we are. But this is not a reason to give up on reconciliation. Rather, God wants to work within our hearts so that we can realize how extensive has been his forgiveness of us as well as demonstrate that same forgiveness to others.

- *Who is the last person you forgave? Who is the last person to have forgiven you? Tell the story.*

- *How difficult is it for you to ask forgiveness from God? From others? Why—or why not—is it so difficult for you?*

- *What is the best way to live in peace with other people?*

 EXPERIENCE GOD'S HEART

Unfortunately, in King David's life, he never experienced resolution of the conflicts with either his son Absalom (who was killed after his hair got tangled in a tree as he fled—see 2 Samuel 18:9–15) or his counselor Ahithophel (who later committed suicide—see 17:23).

- *How difficult is it for you to deal with unresolved conflict? What makes it such a challenge?*

- *What is a believer's responsibility if the person with whom they are in conflict dies?*

Mark Twain once wrote, "Anger is an acid that can do more harm to the vessel in which it is stored than to anything on which it is poured."

- *How can lingering unforgiveness and resentment harm a person? Be as specific as you can.*

- *How would you define forgiveness?*

- *Must forgiveness involve the restoration of the relationship? Why or why not?*

The essence of Psalm 55 is that David places his trust in God to take care of the issues he is having with Absalom and Ahithophel. He makes the conscious choice to trust in God (see v. 23). David essentially declares, *God, you take over for me in this conflict. You do the saving. You bring down the proud in your timing—as you see fit. As for me, I will simply keep my eyes on you.*

David is realistic about the situation. He likely knows that reconciliation won't be taking place—at least not during his time on earth. But he rests in the knowledge that no matter what happens in his human relationships, his relationship with God is rock solid—and that is where he places his hope.

- *How can you allow God's Spirit to so transform you that during times of conflict, your instincts are godly, trending toward forgiveness and peace in your relationships?*

- *Write a prayer to the Lord, acknowledging him as the number one relationship in your life. As difficult as it may be, place your other relationships in his capable hands. If he leads you to take a step toward resolving a conflict—such as writing a note, making a phone call, or simply admitting within your own heart your role in the situation—acknowledge that in your prayer and commit to following through.*

SHARE GOD'S HEART

The Bible goes to great lengths to teach us how we should treat one another, including how to live in peace with one another, how to practice forgiveness, and the importance of reconciliation whenever possible.

- *How can you be a peacemaker in your own world—your family, your workplace, your sphere of influence?*

- *If a relationship with another person needs to be renewed or strengthened, brainstorm ways—no matter how small— to reach out this week and then commit to doing so.*

Talking It Out

1. Many of David's prayers in the book of Psalms—including Psalm 55—are brutally honest. He lays out all of his emotions before God even when his thoughts and feelings trend toward revenge. Is it ever okay to ask God to punish our enemies or those with whom we are in conflict? How did Jesus instruct us to pray for our enemies (see Matthew 5:44–45)? Does this differ from David's perspective? In what ways?

2. Is there a difference between pouring your heart out to God and praying a selfish, self-centered prayer? Why or why not?

3. It has been said that "*anger* is only one letter removed from *danger*." At what point do anger and conflict become dangerous? Explain your answer.

4. What is the most honest prayer you have ever prayed to God? What was the situation? If it was resolved, how did that occur? If no resolution happened, why not?

LESSON 6

Comfort in Times of Sickness

(Psalms 6, 38)

Additional psalm about sickness and healing: 90

Fifteen-year-old Tyler Clarensau struggled to walk down the aisle at the Park Crest Assembly of God in Springfield, Missouri. He wanted to ask for healing for his malformed knee joints. He'd had surgery to correct them, but rather than helping his condition, the surgery had left him worse than before, with swelling and intense pain.

At the front of the church, a group of fellow believing teenagers gathered around Tyler and began to pray for him as the rest of the people in the congregation joined their prayers to those of the kids. They prayed for Tyler for forty-five minutes until, finally, a hush fell on the group. One of the members of the congregation stood and boldly stated that God had healed Tyler of his condition.

Although nothing had yet taken place in Tyler's body, he unsteadily rose to his feet. He had not walked correctly in years, let alone done knee bends, but as he began to move his legs, he suddenly found himself able to do just that: deep knee bends, then walking, even running around the church.

Ever since that day, Tyler has been able to walk and run with no trouble in his knee joints. "I heard about people getting healed," he said. "I thought it was pretty cool. But I didn't know for sure about such healing until it happened to me."[24]

When someone is sick or needs physical healing, nothing else will do. No amount of money in this world can buy good health— but the good news is that Jesus purchased healing for us on the cross. As the writer of psalms in the Old Testament, King David could only look forward to that time when the Messiah would come, but when he faced intense sickness and disease, he cried out to God for comfort and healing.

You, too, can turn to God when your body needs healing. He is the one who created your body; he certainly knows how to cure it. Let's take a look at David's prayers to the Lord in Psalms 6 and 38, written when he needed healing from sickness, and use his words to come to God and receive comfort and healing when we need it ourselves.

A Cry for Healing

David is sick. We don't know what kind of illness he is experiencing, but he literally feels like his body is falling apart and that he could be nearing death.

• *Read Psalm 6. List as many as you can find of the physical symptoms that David is experiencing in his body.*

- *Have you—or has someone close to you—ever been critically ill (or perhaps you are now)? What was that like for you or for this other person?*

- *Can you relate to David's complaints? What were the similarities and the differences between what he went through and what you experienced?*

David wrote both Psalms 6 and 38 when he was facing physical illness. Bible scholars aren't certain whether he wrote them both around the same time and if they concerned the same illness or whether David faced severe illness several times in his life. Whatever the case, he was familiar with the discouragement, fear, and worry that sickness and pain in his body brought.

- *Read Psalm 38. What kind of symptoms did David face as expressed in this psalm?*

Causes of Illness

People get sick for many reasons. Some people have genetic propensities toward certain diseases that run in their families. Other people persist in bad habits—smoking, an unhealthy diet, a lack of exercise—that can ultimately cause illnesses in their bodies. Of course, the real reason for sickness and disease is the fact that we live in a broken, sinful world. God never wanted it to be this way. He created a perfect garden for Adam and Eve, but their initial sin there opened the door for sickness and death to enter God's beautiful creation.

When Jesus walked on the earth, he healed many people who had all kinds of diseases. However, David lived during Old Testament times, long before Jesus' birth, and his perspective on the cause of his sickness came from the knowledge of God he had at that time.

- *Within the first ten verses of Psalm 38, David mentions his physical agony over twelve times. What does he see as the root cause of his illness?*

In the Old Testament, suffering was typically understood to be caused by sin. Sometimes that is the case; sometimes it is not.

- *Do you know anyone whose illness or injury seemed to be a direct result of sin? What happened?*

- *Sometimes our own sin or that of others is the cause of the injuries and illnesses we experience, but sometimes people suffer from sickness that has no connection to their sin or the sin of another. Why do you think that is the case?*

When Healing Doesn't Come

When sociologist Tony Campolo was in a church in Oregon, he prayed for a man who had cancer. He relates this story.

> In the middle of the week, I received a telephone call, and it was [the sick man's] wife. And she said, "You prayed for my husband. He had cancer."
>
> I said, "Had?" *Whoa*, I thought, *it's happened.* [*He's been healed.*]
>
> She said, "He died." I felt terrible.
>
> She said, "Don't feel bad. When he came into that church that Sunday, he was filled with anger. He knew he was going to be dead in a short period of time, and he hated God. He was fifty-eight years old.

He wanted to see his children grow up and his grandchildren grow up, and he was angry that this God did not take away his sickness and heal him. He would lie in bed and curse God. The more his anger grew toward God, the more miserable he was to everybody around him. It was an awful thing to be in his presence.

"And you prayed for him, and when he left that church, a peace had come over him and a joy had come into him...The last three days have been the best days of our lives. We've sung. We've laughed. We've read Scripture. We prayed. Oh, they've been wonderful days. And I called to thank you for laying your hands on him and praying for healing."

And then she said something incredibly profound...She said, "He wasn't cured, but he was healed."[25]

• *In Psalm 6:5, David asked God, "How could I bring you praise if I'm buried in a tomb?" Was this a legitimate question for him to ask? Have you ever asked God a question like this before? If so, what was the situation?*

- *What does this question tell you about David's relationship with God?*

- *The final verses of Psalm 6 indicate that David's prayer for healing was answered (vv. 8–10). However, Psalm 38 ends with David pleading that God would hurry to help him (v. 22) because his ill condition remains unchanged (v. 21). God may have ultimately healed David, but the psalm leaves open God's response. What have you typically done when God has answered your prayer? What has been your response when his answer didn't come right away or perhaps not at all?*

- *The gravesites of believers show that God does not heal everyone all the time on this side of heaven. Why do you think this is so? If someone asked you to explain your answer, what reasons would you give to support it?*

 EXPERIENCE GOD'S HEART

Read Psalm 6 again.

- *When David asks for healing, does he appeal to his own character or to the character of God? Why?*

- *To what characteristics of God does he appeal?*

- *What does this tell you about God's character as related to your own healing?*

- *What do you believe God wants to do for you with respect to healing?*

Even though David is grappling with the *why* question of his illness, these psalms ultimately do not answer that question. Even when God provides healing for David, he still does not explain why David suffered. Instead, God shows him mercy in Psalm 6, while in Psalm 38, we don't learn what God did for David. But isn't that what mercy is? It is not expected, but it is often granted. It cannot be demanded, but it can be freely offered. Mercy from God is always his prerogative to give or withhold. And because he is infinitely good and wise, we can rest assured that whatever he chooses to do will ultimately be for our good.

- *How has God shown you mercy in the past?*

- *How is God showing mercy to you now, including in the midst of your own struggles, health problems, or something else altogether?*

♥ SHARE GOD'S HEART

Psalm 38 shares David's hurt after people rejected him due to his illness. Some Bible scholars believe they were probably following Levitical law regarding illness. For example, in Leviticus 13:45–46 (NIV), God gives commands regarding the treatment of those with infectious diseases:

> Anyone with such a defiling disease [such as reddish-white, swollen sores on the skin] must wear torn clothes, let their hair be unkempt, cover the lower part of their face and cry out, "Unclean! Unclean!" As long as they have the disease they remain unclean. They must live alone; they must live outside the camp.

• *Why do you think God might have put these rules in place?*

• *Are they still applicable to Christians today? Why or why not?*

Whether people were simply obeying the law, were rejecting David because they believed he was experiencing God's punishment, or were acting this way due to some other reason, David still felt the sting of rejection—at a time when he most needed the emotional support of other people.

• *Has anyone ever turned away from you when you experienced a difficult time in your life—whether it was due to sickness or some other hardship? What happened? How did you feel?*

- *Whom do you know today who is dealing with a health problem or sickness? What are some ways you can reach out to them this week and remind them of God's love and faithfulness in the midst of their suffering?*

Talking It Out

1. Psalms 6 and 38 indicate that some people were actually glad that David was suffering. Have you had people in your life who delighted over your pain? What direction do these psalms provide for how to deal with such people?

2. Do you have any theories about what illness David was experiencing? What are his symptoms? How are they similar or dissimilar to those you or a loved one has experienced? Is there any illness that is too difficult for God to heal? Why or why not?

3. Why do some people avoid those who go through tough times, preferring instead to spend time with those for whom everything seems to be going well? Why do other people rush to help those who are suffering? Which type of person are you? Which type of person would you like to be?

LESSON 7

Comfort When You Need Forgiveness

(Psalm 32)

Additional psalms about sin and forgiveness: 25, 51, 103, 143

There is a commonly told anecdote about sixteenth-century theologian Martin Luther, who went to sleep one night troubled about his sin. In a dream he had that night, he saw an angel standing by a wall, and at the top of the wall was Luther's name. On the wall, the angel was writing out all of Luther's sins, one by one, until the wall was filled with a record of his transgressions. Luther shuddered in despair, feeling that his sins were so many that he would never be forgiven. But then, suddenly, in the dream he saw a pierced hand writing these words above the list: "The blood of Jesus Christ His Son cleanses us from all sin." As Luther gazed on in amazement, the blood flowed out of the wounded hand and washed the wall clean. No record of his sins remained.[26]

Sin. It's part of the human condition in our fallen world. The Bible says that all of us have sinned: "We all have sinned and are in need of the glory of God" (Romans 3:23).

The worst part of sin is that it separates us from God. Even as believers, sin harms the relationship we have with him. In Psalm 66, the writer realized that if he had ignored his sin, "the Lord God would have closed his ears to my prayer" (v. 18). Unconfessed sin can close us off from divine blessing and answers. A well-known saying admonishes us to "keep our accounts short with

God." When we repent as David did in Psalm 32, we keep our accounts short with God, and our prayers—and our relationship with him—will be unhindered.

- *If you have unconfessed sin in your life, how might it hinder your relationship with God? What about the people who were affected by your sin?*

- *What happens to your sense of peace and well-being when you have unconfessed sin in your heart and life?*

 THE BACKSTORY

Psalm 32 is one of a group of psalms called the psalms of confession, or penitential psalms. This group includes Psalms 6, 32, 38, 51, 102, 130, and 143. All these psalms reflect an emotional response that King David had to a sin he had committed. Psalms 32 and 51 were both written after David was confronted by the prophet Nathan after his sin of adultery with Bathsheba, which soon turned into murder when David sent her husband, Uriah, into battle so he would be killed and David's sin would not be discovered.

- *Read 2 Samuel 11–12. At what point did David feel remorse for his sin? Why do you suppose he didn't feel sorrow over what he had done until that point? What words of Nathan's got through to David's heart?*

After the admonishment by the prophet Nathan, David felt deeply remorseful over his personal sin, and through Psalms 32 and 51, he demonstrates to us what genuine repentance looks like.

- *What would you consider the most important quality of genuine repentance? Why do you name this characteristic? Why is it important to you?*

Three Types of Sin

According to the translator of Psalm 32 in The Passion Translation, "David uses three Hebrew words to describe sin in these first two verses: 'rebellion,' 'sins' (failures, falling short), and 'corruption' (crookedness, the twisting of right standards)."[27]

- *Can you give examples of each of these types of sins in our society today?*

- *Which of these three types of sins most affects your life? Why do you think this is true?*

- *According to Psalm 32:6, at what point should believers confess their sins?*

- *What part does the Holy Spirit play in "uncovering" or "exposing" our sins? Has he ever moved on your own heart in this way? What happened?*

- *Have you personally followed the instruction of Psalm 32:6? If so, what was the result?*

Genuine Repentance Brings Forgiveness

Most people understand that there is a very real difference between genuine, heartfelt repentance of sin and just apologizing but not changing your behavior or only being sorry "you got caught." Genuine repentance involves admitting your personal sin, being remorseful for it, and then changing your ways.

Pastor and author Roger Barrier tells the story of learning an important lesson about doing laundry. Before heading out on his own, Barrier—like many young men—had never done his own laundry. His mother took care of the chore for him, and before he left for college, his mother gave him a canvas duffle bag, saying, "Put your dirty clothes in this every night…At the end of the week, wash them at the Laundromat."

After his first week at college, Roger did as he was told. He grabbed the duffel full of dirty clothes and hauled it over to the campus laundromat. When completing the task, he put the entire duffel bag into the coin-operated washing machine, poured in laundry detergent, put in his coins, and turned on the machine. Not long after, a jarring *thump*, *thump*, *thump* could be heard throughout the laundromat. The sound attracted the attention of a pretty girl. "I watched you load your washer," she said, smiling. "I think the clothes would get cleaner if you took them out of the bag."

Later on in life, Roger's relationship with God was suffering, and he thought back to that time in the laundromat. He realized that when he spoke to the Lord about his sins, he took a similar approach to how he'd washed his first load of dirty clothes: "Dear God, please forgive me for all the sins I've committed today." An ineffective, lumped-together load. He realized that if he truly wanted to come clean to the Lord, he needed to address each sin individually, bringing each one before God, confessing it, and repenting of it. In that way, genuine repentance will more likely be the result.[28]

- How is confessing individual sin better than praying a blanket prayer for forgiveness of all your sins? How might the heart attitude be different in each prayer?

- Psalm 32:1 says, "What bliss belongs to the one whose rebellion has been forgiven, those whose sins are covered by blood." While David was referring to the blood of sacrificed animals in the Old Testament approach to worship, whose blood does this verse foreshadow? Why is blood necessary for our forgiveness? Why do we no longer need to sacrifice animals to satisfy God's justice? (For help, see Hebrews 10:1–18.)

- *How might the confession/acknowledgment of individual sin be an antidote against hypocrisy?*

False Guilt

When we commit a sin, we should feel legitimate guilt. It is much like pain in the body operating as a symptom pointing to a deeper problem that needs to be tended to. Legitimate guilt is good when it leads us to the confession of sin. However, after we have acknowledged our sin and repented, we should no longer feel that sense of guilt.

- *Have you ever had lingering guilt over something you did, even after you were forgiven? How was that guilt resolved?*

The Christian psychiatrist Dr. David Seamands once wrote: "There is no forgiveness from God unless you freely forgive your brother from your heart. And I wonder if we have been too narrow in thinking that 'brother' only applies to someone else. What if you are the brother or sister who needs to be forgiven, and you need to forgive yourself?"[29]

- *What do you think about this statement? Could the command to forgive "your brother" extend to forgiving "yourself"?*

Dr. Paul Brand, writing with Philip Yancey, told a story about his medical school administrator, a man named Mr. Barwick, who had a serious and painful circulation problem in his leg but refused to allow amputation. Finally, the pain became too great for him to bear, and Barwick cried at last, "I'm through with that leg. Take it off."

Surgery was scheduled immediately, but before the operation, Barwick asked the doctor, "What do you do with legs after they're removed?"

"We may take a biopsy or explore them a bit, but afterward we incinerate them."

"I would like you to preserve my leg in a pickling jar," Mr.

Barwick said, to the surprise of all. "I will install it on my mantel shelf. Then, as I sit in my armchair, I will taunt that leg: 'Ha! You can't hurt me anymore!'"

Ultimately Mr. Barwick got his wish, but the despised leg had the last laugh.

Mr. Barwick suffered phantom limb pain of the worst degree. Somehow locked in his memory were the sensations associated with that leg. Even after the wound healed, Mr. Barwick could feel the tortuous pressure of the swelling as the muscles cramped and itched and throbbed.

"He had hated the leg with such intensity that the pain had unaccountably lodged permanently in his brain," wrote Brand, who then added, "To me, phantom limb pain provides wonderful insight into the phenomenon of false guilt. Christians can be obsessed by the memory of some sin committed years ago. It never leaves them, crippling their ministry, their devotional life, their relationships with others...Unless they experience the truth of 1 John 3:19–20 that 'God is greater than our conscience,' they become as pitiful as poor Mr. Barwick, shaking his fist in fury at the pickled leg on the mantel."[30]

- *How difficult is it for you to forgive yourself even after God has forgiven you?*

- *Do you have a "pickled leg on the mantel"? If so, what is it? How might you begin to release it and gain the freedom that God wants you to have?*

 WORD WEALTH

What bliss belongs to the one whose rebellion has been forgiven, those whose sins are covered by blood. (Psalm 32:1)

- *This verse is a favorite memory verse of many people. Why do you think it strikes a chord with so many believers?*

- *Which verse of Psalm 32 is your favorite? Why? If possible, consider memorizing it over the next few days to remind yourself of God's loving mercy and forgiveness.*

 DIGGING DEEPER

According to The Passion Translation study notes for Psalm 32, this was the favorite psalm of Saint Augustine, one of the greatest theologians of the Christian faith. Augustine loved this psalm so much that he asked for it to be written on the wall near his deathbed so he could meditate upon its words.[31]

- *Why do you suppose someone nearing death would find comfort in this psalm?*

- *How are the words of Psalm 32 relevant to every person everywhere?*

 EXPERIENCE GOD'S HEART

I hear the Lord saying, "I will stay close to you, instructing and guiding you along the pathway for your life.
I will advise you along the way
and lead you forth with my eyes as your guide.
So don't make it difficult; don't be stubborn
when I take you where you've not been before.
Don't make me tug you and pull you along.
Just come with me!" (vv. 8–9)

- *In this quoted portion of Psalm 32, what does God promise to do in response to our heartfelt prayer of repentance?*

- *What does he want us to do in return?*

- *Why should actions always follow words when it comes to confessing and repenting of sin?*

- *Have you ever been stubborn when God tries to do something new in your life or lead you in a different direction? How has he "tugged" you or "pulled you along"? How much easier would it be if you would just go with him as he asks?*

- *David's conclusion is found in verses 10–11. Write out these verses below in your own words.*

- *What emotions rise up in your heart as you read and write out these words?*

♥ SHARE GOD'S HEART

Mandisa Hundley, now a famous Christian vocal artist, was one of the twelve finalists on American Idol nearly fifteen years ago. As the story goes:

> When she met with judges Simon Cowell, Paula Abdul, and Randy Jackson to find out if she had made it through to the next round of the competition, however, she got a stinging comment from Simon—the judge best known for his snarky, yet somewhat truthful, remarks.
>
> Eyeing Mandisa, who was heavyset, Simon asked, "Do we have a bigger stage this year?"
>
> When she entered the room to learn the judges' verdict, Mandisa looked directly at Simon and said, "Simon, a lot of people want me to say a lot of things to you. But this is what I want to say: Yes, you hurt me, and I cried, and it was painful. But I want you to know that I've forgiven you, and that you don't need someone to apologize to forgive somebody. And I figure that if Jesus could die so that all of my wrongs could be forgiven, I can certainly extend that same grace to you. I just wanted you to know that."
>
> Simon apologized and hugged the singer, and Mandisa discovered that she had advanced to the next round.[32]

Aside from the discovery of a great singer, the episode revealed an even more profound truth: when we have been forgiven much by God, we also have a duty to forgive other people.

- *Who needs your forgiveness today?*

- *Of whom do you need to ask forgiveness?*

- *Make a plan to seek out these important conversations within the next few days.*

Talking It Out

1. When someone else has sinned against you or harmed you in some way, is true reconciliation of the relationship possible if that person never acknowledges the harm he or she has caused? Expand that thought to your relationship with God. Is a restoration of our relationship with him possible without confessing and acknowledging our sin?

2. David experienced significant physical problems when he was grievously repentant for his sin. What symptoms did he have (Psalm 32:3–4)? How does what we feel in our souls and our spirits affect what we experience in our bodies?

3. Read Psalm 51, the companion to Psalm 32. What are the similarities and differences you see between the two psalms? How do these psalms work together to paint a picture of a repentant man or woman? How do they point the way for us to restore our own relationship with God and with other people?

LESSON 8

Comfort in a World Gone Wrong

(Psalm 58)

Additional psalms about a world gone wrong: 70, 71, 83

The Bible presents a God who is absolute perfection, who is a God of love, and yet who is simultaneously a God of wrath. A. T. Pierson compares it to an arch. You have the love of God supporting one side and the wrath of God supporting the other side, and without either of them, the entire thing would fall down. God would not be God if he didn't have the capacity for wrath.[33]

Consider. There once was a young, handsome, dapper fellow, a medical doctor who always wore crisp and well-tailored clothing. He handled himself with polish and smoothness. He always bore the fragrance of expensive cologne. But his very demeanor made him all the more fiendish, for his name was Josef Mengele, the Angel of Death at Auschwitz, which was the most infamous concentration camp in all of Nazi Germany. With a flick of his well-washed and perfumed hand, Mengele personally selected four hundred thousand prisoners to die in the gas chamber. He conducted horrible experiments on people, hoping to produce a superior race. One observer said, "He would spend hours bent over his microscope while the air outside stank with the heavy odor of burning flesh from the chimney stacks of the crematoria."

He had a special fascination for children who were twins. He would give them horrible injections, operate on their spines to paralyze them, then begin removing parts of their body one at a time for observation.[34]

If God could sit back and watch this sort of indescribable evil without feeling any anger, what kind of God would he be? If God could simply observe the pain, the evil, and the injustice in this world with no feelings of indignation, he would be among the most immoral beings in the universe. Actually, he wouldn't be God at all. But this is not the way God is. Scripture is clear: God hates evil (Proverbs 6:16–19; Isaiah 61:8), and he will bring about justice (Acts 17:31; Romans 2:5–6). He is immutably just (Psalm 89:14), holy (99:9), and wrathful (Romans 1:18; 2:5). "'Vengeance is mine, and I will repay,' says the Lord" (Romans 12:19). We can count on this.

Still, evil is here, and sometimes it seems to succeed better than good does. David wrestled with the evil that is still in this world, and we might also wonder where God's justice is when it seems egregious sin and corruption are running rampant. For justice may at times exercise mercy, but there's no genuine mercy without the expectation of punishment, even wrathful punishment.

David prayed a prayer in Psalm 58 that we can pray as well today—a prayer to the Lord when we are seeking his comfort in a world gone wrong.

Getting Justice Right

- *First, read Psalm 58. If you can, read it aloud, even adding the emotional punch that emanates from David's words.*
- *Return to verses 1 through 5 and answer the questions that follow:*

   Who claims to know what God's justice is?

Does David believe that these leaders know what true justice is? What are David's indictments against these leaders and their brand of justice?

Do you see leaders today who have earned any or all of David's accusations? Cite some examples.

Have you ever been on the receiving end of such injustice or been a witness to it? Tell about your experience.

• *Now review verses 6 through 9. What actions does David call out for God to take against these unjust leaders?*

- *Have you ever asked God to punish the doers of injustice? What were the circumstances? Did God answer your prayer, and if so, what happened?*

- *Turn now to verses 10 and 11. What does David believe that followers of God will do once he carries out his divine justice? What conclusions will they draw from God's just actions?*

- *If God has corrected an injustice in your life or in the life of someone you know, in what ways did that influence your view of God and even your relationship with him?*

🎬 THE BACKSTORY

Bible scholars refer to Psalm 58 as an imprecatory psalm, or a "psalm of cursing." (Some other imprecatory psalms are Psalms 35, 69, 109, and 140. Consider reading these additional psalms for context.) Imprecatory psalms contain appeals for justice and vindication. They are filled with raw emotion. They help us express our frustration and indignation to God when we see things going wrong in the world or when we are wronged personally. When we read the words of David in Psalm 58, they can help us process our own emotions with honesty and truth, with faith in God and hope that he will ensure that true justice will have the final word.

While called imprecatory psalms, it's more accurate to say that these psalms include calls for justice to fall upon the wicked in certain ways while also affirming and even worshiping God as righteous, just, caring, and redemptive.[35] They are written by followers of God who love what is good and hate what is evil, who love what God loves and hate what he hates. In Scripture, love and hate are not antithetical as long as one loves what should be loved and hates what should be hated. We should always love what is good and hate what is evil. Moreover, we must support those who love the good, and we must oppose those who love evil.

- *Look up each passage that follows, and next to each write what you learn about good and evil and how we should act in relation to good and evil:*

  Deuteronomy 16:18–22

  Psalm 5:4–6, 11–12

  Proverbs 6:16–18

  Proverbs 11:27

  Isaiah 1:16–17

  Matthew 12:33–37

  Luke 6:35–36

  John 3:16–21

Romans 12:17–21

Romans 15:1–2

Romans 16:19

Galatians 6:7–10

Titus 3:8–11

3 John 11

- *Did you learn anything about good and evil, love and hate that you didn't already know? If so, what?*

Justice vs. Injustice

Justice, like all else that is morally right and good, is rooted in God. He is the Source of justice because he himself is inherently just. Another word for *justice* in Scripture is *righteousness*. The New Testament Greek term for "righteous" is *dikaios*, which means "to be just" or "right." The Bible affirms that the foundation of God's throne is righteousness (Psalm 89:14), he rules in righteousness and cherishes it while detesting lawlessness (Hebrews 1:8–9), and he is righteous and never does anything wrong (Zephaniah 3:5). In other words, God is "absolutely just or right and is the ultimate standard of justice and rightness."[36] Part of his righteous judgment is to "give to each one [person] in return for what he has done" (Romans 2:6). For those who do good, which is always pleasing to our just God, their ultimate destiny is eternal life. But for "those governed by selfishness and self-promotion, whose hearts are unresponsive to God's truth and would rather embrace unrighteousness," they will ultimately experience the "fullness of [God's] wrath" (v. 8).

Human beings may pass laws and base what is just on those, but if those laws do not accord with God's standard of justice, then they are unjust. God is the measure of justice, not humanity.

We should strive to live our lives in light of what God deems good, true, and right. When we do, we will more clearly see when the world goes wrong and why. And we will stand as living witnesses to what is genuine, true, just, and good. This will give us comfort and peace within even if we face antagonism and persecution for taking our stand on God's side. In the end, he will vindicate *us*, not those who have opposed him by shaking their fists at us (12:19).

- *Look up the following passages. Next to each one, record what it reveals about God's just righteousness, how it relates to us, and how we should live in light of it:*

Matthew 5:6

Matthew 6:33

Romans 6:18

Romans 10:1–4

1 Peter 3:13–17

1 John 3:7–8

The Just Way to Live at Peace

To live at peace with ourselves and with God requires that we live justly, rightly. Our lives need to line up with God and what he wants for us. We cannot do this on our own strength or according to our own wisdom, which is why God delivers us from evil through the death of his Son, Jesus Christ, empowers us to fight against evil and grow in goodness through the indwelling work of his Spirit, and gives us the clarity of his written Word so we can grow in our discernment of good and evil and learn better how to live for him, in him, and through him. True freedom does not consist in doing anything we want but in voluntarily living according to what God wants for us. And this will always be a life that is just and right.

In Galatians, Paul contrasts two ways of living. The life to self bears unrighteous fruit: "Sexual immorality, lustful thoughts, pornography, chasing after things instead of God, manipulating others, hatred of those who get in your way, senseless arguments, resentment when others are favored, temper tantrums, angry quarrels, only thinking of yourself, being in love with your own opinions, being envious of the blessings of others, murder, uncontrolled addictions, wild parties, and all other similar behavior." But living to God through the work of his Spirit produces "divine love in all its varied expressions: joy that overflows, peace that subdues, patience that endures, kindness in action, a life full of virtue, faith that prevails, gentleness of heart, and strength of spirit" (Galatians 5:19–23). Which way do you want to live? How do you want to use your freedom in Christ? Do you really want to live justly or unjustly?

Now, living God's way will not keep you from persecution, slander, and other forms of opposition and challenge. We live in a fallen world. Evil has plunged our world into darkness—a darkness that shrinks from and rages against the Light. This Light is Jesus the Messiah, and while he "never fails to shine through darkness" and darkness cannot overcome him (John 1:5), darkness declared the innocent Light guilty and nailed him to a cross to extinguish him. But the Light rose from the grave, conquering death and darkness, and later ascended into heaven until that day the Light will return to judge the darkness forever and banish it from his presence and the presence of those who have joined with the Light through faith. Until that day of judgment, darkness fights on, hoping against hope that it can still win a war that Christ has won already. We live on the earthly battlefield of this war, and we cannot avoid engaging in it, which is why Paul calls on us to clothe ourselves with God's armor and fight with the weapons he has given us (Ephesians 6:10–20). We must stand strong against evil and injustice no matter the forms they take.

- *What injustices do you see going on in today's world?*

- *God is far from passive when it comes to injustice. How can we be an advocate for those who are treated unjustly?*

- *David's rebuke of injustice in this psalm was public. In what ways are we called today to publicly rebuke unjust and ungodly people? How can we do so in a godly way?*

Praying for God to Intervene

Most people—even nonbelievers—long for justice to be served when we hear of unjust happening in our world. When King David pleads with God to go against evil-doers, we can join in his prayer—and prayer is one of the most effective strategies to defeat the enemy.

In Psalm 57:6, David writes the following words: "They have set a trap for me. Frantic fear has me overwhelmed. But look! The very trap they set for me has sprung shut upon themselves instead of me!"

- *In prayer, we can ask God to break the power of corrupt leaders to do damage in the world. And he often does that by permitting the wicked plans they have for others to boomerang and entrap them. How have you seen that happen? As far as you can tell, what has been its impact on those who tried to undermine others and take them down?*

The damage that corrupt leaders can do in our society isn't something to be taken lightly or dismissed. David compares these evil leaders to "cobras" waiting to strike (58:5) and "lions" seeking to tear others to shreds (57:4). And just as the king of Persia praised God after Daniel's life was spared in the lions' den many years after David's reign, "the godly will celebrate in the triumph of good over evil" (58:10).

The ultimate lesson here is that in our prayers, we must plead with God as if the stakes are high in our world—because they are!

In addition to asking the Lord to break the power of corrupt politicians, we can also ask him to remove them from office completely (58:7–9).

Jesus' attitude toward corrupt leaders who take advantage of the common people can be seen in the Gospel accounts of his life:

> Upon entering Jerusalem Jesus went directly
> into the temple area and drove away all the
> merchants who were buying and selling their
> goods. He overturned the tables of the money
> changers and the stands of those selling doves.
> And he said to them, "My dwelling place will be
> known as a house of prayer, but you have made
> it into a hangout for thieves!" (Matthew 21:12–13)

Jesus was especially incensed because some of the leaders of the society in which he lived were religious leaders. They were the representatives of God to the people and should have known better than to exploit their position to profit themselves.

The principle at work then is the same for our world today. Power corrupts, as they say, and absolute power corrupts absolutely. When political—or religious—leaders get a taste of power, wealth, or fame, it often becomes too great of a temptation to use their power and influence to gain even more.

- *Jesus demonstrated righteous anger toward the corrupt religious leaders of his day. How can our attitude and actions toward corrupt leaders in our own time reflect his righteous anger? Is it possible to take that anger too far?*

- *What can you do today to promote righteousness and take a stand against corruption in your society? Make a call to your congressman or start a petition for a righteous cause? Summon your courage to engage in a "political" conversation with friends or colleagues? Support a charity or church that has come under fire because it won't buckle under unjust criticism or comply with unjust demands? Ask God to guide and inspire you to stand up for him and his righteousness in order to make a difference in the lives of others.*

God's Final Justice

Ultimately, God will reign throughout all eternity in justice and peace. Consider the following passages of Scripture:

> God exalted [Jesus] and multiplied his greatness! He has now been given the greatest of all names!
> The authority of the name of Jesus causes every knee to bow in reverence! Everything and everyone will one day

submit to this name—in the heavenly realm, in the earthly realm, and in the demonic realm. And every tongue will proclaim in every language: "Jesus Christ is Lord Yahweh," bringing glory and honor to God, his Father! (Philippians 2:9–11)

The seventh angel sounded his trumpet, and a loud voice broke forth in heaven, saying: "The kingdom of the world has become the kingdom of our God and of his Anointed One! He will reign supreme for an eternity of eternities!" (Revelation 11:15)

I saw heaven opened, and suddenly a white horse appeared. The name of the one riding it was Faithful and True, and with pure righteousness he judges and rides to battle. He wore many regal crowns, and his eyes were flashing like flames of fire. He had a secret name inscribed on him that's known only to himself. He wore a robe dipped in blood, and his title is called the Word of God. Following him on white horses were the armies of heaven, wearing white fine linen, pure and bright. A sharp sword came from his mouth with which to conquer the nations, and he will shepherd them with an iron scepter. He will trample out the wine in the winepress of the wrath of God. On his robe and on his thigh he had inscribed a name: King of kings and Lord of lords. (Revelation 19:11–16)

- *What do these verses of Scripture have to say about God's ultimate triumph over evil? When will this triumph take place? Who will execute this judgment of God?*

- *When many people think of Jesus, they think of him as only being kind, humble, and meek. How do these verses challenge that perception?*

When Jesus was on the earth, he responded to his disciples' request for him to teach them "how to pray" with a model prayer that most of us know by heart: the Lord's Prayer. Here it is in The Passion Translation:

> Our Beloved Father, dwelling in the heavenly realms,
> may the glory of your name
> be the center on which our lives turn.
> Manifest your kingdom realm,
> and cause your every purpose to be fulfilled on earth,
> just as it is in heaven.
> We acknowledge you as our Provider
> of all we need each day.
> Forgive us the wrongs we have done as we ourselves
> release forgiveness to those who have wronged us.
> Rescue us every time we face tribulation
> and set us free from evil.
> For you are the King who rules
> with power and glory forever.
> Amen. (Matthew 6:9–13)

- *How does praying the first few lines of the Lord's Prayer invite God to move in our world?*

- *How does the phrase "set us free from evil" relate to David's prayer in Psalm 58?*

- *How might the last few lines of the Lord's Prayer encourage believers that God has the ability to execute justice on the earth?*

• *How do these passages of Scripture bring you hope?*

What Can I Do?

The film *Schindler's List* chronicled the heroic efforts of a German industrialist named Oskar Schindler. Through his unselfish activities, over a thousand Jews on the trains to Auschwitz were saved. Although the film, even on television, has some very graphic and disturbing scenes, the message itself is profound.

After Oskar Schindler discovered what was happening at Auschwitz, he began a systematic effort to save as many Jews as he could. For money, he could buy Jews to work in his factory, which was supposed to be a part of the military machine of Germany. On the one hand, he was buying as many Jews as he could, and on the other hand, he was deliberately sabotaging the ammunition produced in his factory that was supposed to help advance Germany's military. He entered World War II as a wealthy industrialist; by the end of the war, he was basically bankrupt.

When the Germans surrendered, Schindler met with his workers and declared that at midnight they were all free to go. The most emotional scene of the film is when Schindler says goodbye to the financial manager of the plant, a Jew and his good and trusted friend. As he embraces his friend, Schindler sobs and says, "I could have done more." He looks at his automobile and asks, "Why did I save this? I could have bought ten Jews with this." Taking out another small possession, he cries, "This would have saved another one. Why didn't I do more?"

- *Can you think of other examples from history or the present of individuals or groups, especially Christian ones, who have risked careers, reputations, finances, relationships, and even their lives to help others face and overcome injustice? Record at least one example that's especially meaningful to you.*

EXPERIENCE GOD'S HEART

It is important to remember that we are all sinners; our own unredeemed selves are really no better than those of corrupt politicians.

Paul wrote the following words in Romans 3. Interestingly, he was quoting from different passages of the Old Testament in this passage:

> There is no one who always does what is right,
> no, not even one!
> There is no one with true spiritual insight,
> and there is no one who seeks after God alone.
> All have deliberately wandered from God's ways.

All have become depraved and unfit.
Kindness has disappeared from them all,
not even one is good.
Their words release a stench,
like the smell of death—foul and filthy!
Deceitful lies roll off their tongues.
The venom of a viper drips from their lips.
Bitter profanity flows from their mouths,
only meant to cut and harm.
They are infatuated with violence and murder.
They release ruin and misery wherever they go.
They never experience the path of peace.
They shut their eyes to the awe-inspiring God!
(vv. 10–18)

- *Note the similarities between Paul's words here in
  Romans 3 and David's prayer in Psalm 58. How are
  these passages of Scripture alike?*

- *While David was writing about corrupt politicians in his day, Paul extended the description of corruption and depravity to every single person who has ever lived. What does this comparison tell you about human nature apart from God's redemptive work?*

- *How has trusting in Jesus for salvation and allowing the Holy Spirit to change your heart made you different from those about whom David was writing in Psalm 58?*

- *Write a prayer to the Lord, thanking him for his salvation. How wonderful it is to have been brought over into the kingdom of light, the kingdom of God's dear Son!*

SHARE GOD'S HEART

God calls us to live in peace with all people—as much as we possibly can—and to love our neighbors as ourselves. We should never think of ourselves as better than anyone else because we believe we are right on political or cultural issues. A good dose of humility and an open-hearted, listening ear can go a long way toward bringing peace in our world—starting with our "neighbors," those who are closest to us in the circles in which we travel.

- *Do you know someone who is a member of a different political party or who holds political views different from your own? Make it a point this week to reach out to them, setting politics aside, and share what God is doing in your life.*

- *The greatest way to find comfort in a world gone awry is to offer the gospel to those who need it. The more people who come to know Christ and live according to his light, the less evil there will be to challenge and the more believers there will be to challenge what remains. With whom can you share the gospel? What the world needs most are Jesus Christ and his righteousness.*

Talking It Out

1. In order to act with justice, we must know what is morally right and what is morally wrong. Discuss one or more of the issues of today and seek to answer as best you can what is the morally right view to take and the reasons you have to support your conclusion. Name-calling and slanderous labels (e.g., racist, homophobic, transphobic, xenophobic, and extremist) are not reasons but the absence of reasons. They are reminiscent of children pointing fingers at one another and calling each other names on the playground while never fairly and with any genuine evidence backing up their words and actions. We must do much better. What are the facts of the matter, not just the claims? Can you provide any evidential support from God's Word for your view? What have other godly Christians said and done? What else should you consider as part of your discussion? Do your best to think and reason as Christ, rising above the vitriol and accusations that so often characterize exchanges on cultural, ethical, and political issues today.

2. As a Christian, is it ever okay to disobey the law to protest injustice in a society? For example, some pro-life groups who protest outside of abortion clinics break civil laws in an attempt to save the lives of unborn children and help the mothers who see abortion as their only way out. What does God call us to do in such situations? Are there any stories and principles in Scripture that can provide us with some guidance? Explain your answer.

3. Many people feel free to unleash vitriolic language and comments on social media against what they see as egregious wrongs in our society. How can we be critics of the things we see wrong in the world and still respond with the character of Christ?

LESSON 9

Comfort When God Seems Distant

(Psalm 11)

Additional psalms about feeling God is distant: 22, 27, 42

The beloved hymn "Great Is Thy Faithfulness" was written by a man named Thomas Chisholm, who, much like the great US president Abraham Lincoln, was born in a log cabin in Kentucky. When Chisholm was a young adult, he came to faith in Jesus due to the evangelist H. C. Morrison. Thomas Chisholm's health was not good—he went back and forth between bouts of serious illness, in which he could not work at all, and times of great productivity, when he worked as a journalist, an insurance broker, and even an evangelist. During all the turbulent times of his life, he clung to the truth found in Lamentations 3, and the hymn he wrote reflected those words, which had become precious to him.

Not many people had ever heard the hymn, however, until it was popularized by the singer George Beverly Shea at the televised Billy Graham crusades in the 1950s.

Wilber Konkel attended a Billy Graham crusade in 1954. This man had fought in World War II, and when he heard the words sung by Shea, "Great is Thy faithfulness, Lord, unto me," the dark nights of the war returned to his mind. "Each night [in London]," he wrote, "as the enemy planes came over, we cast our care upon the Lord. I quoted Lamentations 3 to myself over and over. I used it in my prayers. Those were dark days. At times they seemed hopeless. It was in those darkest hours that God proved His faithfulness to me. We were so near death. Yet it is because of the Lord's mercies that we are not consumed, because His compassions fail not. They are new every morning."[37]

Sometimes in dark days, God seems hard to find. It's as if, like Elvis, God has "left the building," and we are left bewildered and confused by the crises we face, feeling lost and alone.

The good news is that, despite how we may *feel*, feelings aren't facts. The great preacher A. W. Tozer reminds us that God cannot change. "The law of mutation," he wrote, "belongs to a fallen world, but God is immutable, and in Him men of faith find at last eternal performance."[38] He went on to write these comforting words:

> In coming to Him at any time we need
> not wonder whether we shall find Him in
> a receptive mood. He is always receptive
> to misery and need, as well as to love and
> faith. He does not keep office hours nor
> set aside periods when He will see no one.
> Neither does He change His mind about
> anything. Today, this moment, He feels
> toward His creatures, toward babies, toward
> the sick, the fallen, the sinful, exactly as He
> did when He sent His only-begotten Son
> into the world to die for mankind…
> God never changes moods or cools off
> in His affections or loses enthusiasm…"I
> am the Lord, I change not" (Mal. 3:6).[39]

When God seems far away and you can't find his face in the midst of the storm, it is important to remind yourself of the fact that he hasn't changed. Your situation might change, the world around you might change, how you feel about your situation may change, but he never will.

King David experienced fluctuations in his emotions and relationship to God. For example, Psalm 10 begins with a cry to God,

"Lord, why do you seem so far away when evil is near? Why have you hidden yourself when I need you the most?" Then David goes on to describe the attitudes and actions of those individuals and groups who are threatening him and acting wickedly toward God and others (vv. 2–11). David calls on God to arise and judge them, to stop allowing them to have their evil way (vv. 12–18).

Psalm 11, however, begins with David's commitment of steadfast trust in God: "My faith shelters my soul continually in Yahweh" (v. 1). Rather than questioning where God is and why his justice seems delayed, David expresses his trust in God as a constant sheltering presence in his life. David's mood and view have changed.

But if you read through both psalms, you soon realize that while David underwent change, God did not, which is why David found through living with God that he could count on God to stay with him and be for him no matter how he felt and how challenging his situation became. David learned that he could find comfort in God even when God seemed far away and inactive.

- *Reread Psalm 10:1 and the first part of Psalm 11:1. Do either of these passages express where you find yourself with God right now? Explain your answer.*

- *When do you find it easier to trust God? Why is this so?*

- *When does your faith struggle and why?*

 THE BACKSTORY

In Psalm 11, David is in a time of crisis. The foundations of his very life are being threatened (v. 3). Many Bible scholars believe this psalm was written during the time when King Saul was chasing David, when his life was being threatened because of Saul's jealousy of the young David, not because of anything wrong that David had done.

* *How hard is it for you to handle a crisis that you caused yourself? How does this differ from a crisis in your life that someone else has caused, one in which nothing you did wrong played a part?*

* *How do you typically handle these crises?*

Read the following passage of Scripture, taking note of David's treatment of King Saul—the very man who was hunting him as if David were a wild animal, seeking to murder him.

After Saul returned from pursuing the Philistines, he was told, "David is in the Desert of En Gedi." So Saul took three thousand able young men from all Israel and set out to look for David and his men near the Crags of the Wild Goats.

He came to the sheep pens along the way; a cave was there, and Saul went in to relieve himself. David and his men were far back in the cave. The men said, "This is the day the LORD spoke of when he said to you, 'I will give your enemy into your hands for you to deal with as you wish.'" Then David crept up unnoticed and cut off a corner of Saul's robe.

Afterward, David was conscience-stricken for having cut off a corner of his robe. He said to his men, "The LORD forbid that I should do such a thing to my master, the LORD's anointed, or lay my hand on him; for he is the anointed of the LORD." With these words David sharply rebuked his men and did not allow them to attack Saul. And Saul left the cave and went his way.

Then David went out of the cave and called out to Saul, "My lord the king!...See, my father, look at this piece of your robe in my hand! I cut off the corner of your robe but did not kill you. See that there is nothing in my hand to indicate that I am guilty of wrongdoing or rebellion. I have not wronged you, but you are hunting me down to take my life. May the LORD judge

between you and me. And may the LORD
avenge the wrongs you have done to me…"

When David finished saying this,
Saul asked, "Is that your voice, David my
son?" And he wept aloud. "You are more
righteous than I," he said. "You have
treated me well, but I have treated you
badly. You have just now told me about the
good you did to me; the LORD delivered
me into your hands, but you did not kill
me. When a man finds his enemy, does he
let him get away unharmed? May the LORD
reward you well for the way you treated me
today." (1 Samuel 24:1–12, 16–19 NIV)

- *Why did David not take revenge on Saul when he had the
  chance?*

- *Would you have responded in the same way? Why or why not?*

A Matter of Trust

Sometimes we go through things in life that we just don't understand. And sometimes we won't know the answers to our why questions until we reach our heavenly home. But trust isn't trust if we have the answers to all our questions, and faith isn't faith if we have an explanation for everything.

When David went through the crisis he was facing as he wrote Psalm 11, he knew in whom he placed his trust (v. 1), but did he know why some people were after him?

• *Read verses 1–3. What did some of David's supporters advise him to do? Why did they urge him to flee?*

• *Do you see anything in verses 1–3 that indicate why David had enemies who wanted to trap and hurt him? If so, what did you find?*

As Psalm 11 continues, David expresses that his trust in God remains steadfast because "Yahweh is never shaken" (v. 4). David knew God, and what he knew about him sufficed for his trust in him to remain secure.

- *Read verses 4–7. Record below what they tell you about God.*

- *Do you find comfort or more reason to trust in God because of anything David says about him? If so, what stood out to you?*

- *What kinds of comfort do people tend to seek if God seems far away? Which types of comfort are healthy? What types are not?*

- *When you experience crisis, to what or whom do you usually turn?*

- *When was a time you went through a crisis and God seemed very far away? Were you able to trust him for what you needed? How did he come through for you? Tell the story.*

The Advice of Others

Let's revisit the advice David's friends gave him as laid out in verses 1–3.

- *Summarize what his friends told him to do in response to the distress David faced.*

- *Now summarize David's response to them.*

- *No matter how well intentioned, sometimes friends can give us counsel that is not biblically informed, that actually leads us away from trusting God rather than toward resting in and relying on him. Have you had this happen to you? How did you respond to them? What was the result?*

- *Do you have any friends who are spiritually wiser? If so, who are they? How does their counsel typically differ from that of others?*

David's Final Conclusion

When all was said and done, David took his stand on a bedrock truth about God and what those who have committed themselves to him will one day delight in.

- *What was David's conclusion (v. 7)?*

- *How have you seen God's righteousness—his love for what is right and just—play out in your life? In your times of turmoil and crisis?*

♥ EXPERIENCE GOD'S HEART

In an interview with journalist Lee Strobel, Christian philosopher Peter Kreeft concluded that the answer to suffering was "not an answer at all." Instead, he said, "It's the Answerer. It's Jesus himself. It's not a bunch of words; it's *the* Word. It's not a tightly woven philosophical argument; it's a person. *The* person. The answer to suffering cannot just be an abstract idea, because this isn't an abstract issue; it's a personal issue. It requires a personal response. The answer must be someone, not just something, because the issue involves someone—*God, where are you?*"[40]

- *How is the real answer to the question "God, where are you?" answered in the person of Jesus?*

There are numerous comforting phrases to be found in Psalm 11, and these are wonderful reminders of God and his loving care, even if we don't see them at work in our immediate situation.

• *Read each of the following statements and comment on what they mean to you. Which statement speaks to your heart the most strongly? Why? Consider writing out this phrase and placing it on your bathroom mirror or on the wallpaper of your phone so you can read it and meditate on it every day.*

"Yahweh is never shaken" (v. 4).

"[Yahweh is still] reigning…over all" (v. 4).

"[God] closely watches and examines everything man does" and examines "every heart" (v. 4).

"[God's] heavenly rule will prevail over all" (v. 4).

"Yahweh is the Righteous One who loves justice" (v. 7).

"Every godly one will gaze upon his face!" (v. 7).

♥ SHARE GOD'S HEART

• *What is a crisis you have gone through during which you were challenged in your faith but came out stronger in the end?*

• *Is there anyone you know who is going through a similar struggle? If so, who is it? How are they dealing with the crisis?*

Paul wrote in 2 Corinthians 1:4 that we have been comforted by God so we might then be able to comfort other people: "He [God] always comes alongside us to comfort us in every suffering so that we can come alongside those who are in any painful trial. We can bring them this same comfort that God has poured out upon us."

- *What can you do today to bring comfort to that person and the reassurance that God is still in control and has compassion and care for them during their time of crisis?*

Talking It Out

1. Is it possible to be afraid and maintain your trust in God? Explain your answer.

2. Relinquishing our own control over a situation and placing it in God's hands is one of the most challenging things believers are asked to do. Granting that God is in control does not demand that we be passive any more than Jesus sat on his hands while knowing that his Father was looking out for him. So how can we take action to address a situation while also trusting God and placing our lives in his hands?

3. What is your favorite Bible story in which a person of faith was tested? Perhaps they also felt God was distant for a time. How did the story turn out? How does it relate to your own life and circumstances?

LESSON 10

Comfort When You're Discouraged

(Psalm 112)

Additional psalm about discouragement: 13

Glenn Wasson once related a simple experience that had a profound effect on him. He had been clearing brush in the mountains for several hours when he took a lunch break, sat on a log, and bit into his sandwich. The scenery was beautiful—by a rushing stream, woods all around him, a canyon close by.

But his contemplations were broken by a persistent bee that started tormenting him, buzzing around his head, its stinger threatening. Glenn waved it off, but it returned. This time he swatted it to the ground and stepped on it. But to his amazement, the bee emerged from the sand to renew its attack.

This time Glenn ground the insect into the sand, bringing all his 210 pounds to bear. The deed being done, he returned to his log to resume his lunch. But eventually the corner of his eye noticed movement in the sand near his feet. The bee was dragging itself back into the land of the living.

Glenn, intrigued, bent over to watch. The bee's right wing seemed all right, but the left one was "crumpled like a crushed piece of paper." Nonetheless, the bee stretched and tried his wing, moving it slowly up and down. It ran its legs along the length of the damaged wing, trying to straighten it. At the same time, the bee groomed and doctored itself as well as it could, trying to recover from the disaster.

Finally, it tried using its wing, but the left one seemed hopelessly crippled.

Glenn knelt in the sand and bent over for a closer look. Being a veteran pilot, he knew a good deal about wings. He concluded that the bee would never fly again.

The bee, however, had other ideas, and it kept working with its wing, furiously trying to press out the crinkled spots, stretch out the torn spots, and increase the tempo of its fluttering. As Glenn, still on his knees, watched, the bee attempted to fly. It managed an elevation of three inches before crashing back to earth. Undeterred, it tried again and again. Each effort was a little more successful, though sometimes the bee would fly erratically this way or that. At last, the bee took off, buzzed over the stream, and was gone.

"As the bee disappeared," Glenn later wrote, "I realized that I was still on my knees, and I remained on my knees for some time."[41]

Bill Gothard has defined *discouragement* as being "the result of failing a test that we know God brought into our lives."[42] Perhaps it is a test of trusting the Lord when times are tough. Discouragement creeps in when we begin to doubt his faithfulness or his willingness to work on our behalf.

The writer of Psalm 112, titled "The Triumph of Faith," was determined to shake off discouragement and live a life of faith—praising God even in times of darkness:

> Shout in celebration of praise to the Lord!
> Everyone who loves the Lord and delights in him
> will cherish his words and be blessed beyond
> expectation.
> Their descendants will be prosperous and
> influential.
> Every generation of the righteous will experience
> his favor.
> Great blessing and wealth fills the house of the wise,
> for their integrity endures forever.

Even if darkness overtakes them,
sunrise-brilliance will come bursting through
because they are gracious to others, so tender and
true. (Psalm 112:1–4)

- *How is the psalm writer able to maintain such optimism, even in dark circumstances? List as many clues as you can find in these verses.*

Facing Discouragement

One of the greatest theologians of the Christian faith, John Calvin, faced times of serious discouragement in his life and ministry. Consider some of the words he wrote:

- *"I am entangled in so many troublesome affairs that I am almost beside myself."*
- *"You can scarcely believe what a burden of troublesome business I am weighed down and oppressed by here."*
- *"In addition to the immense troubles by which I am so sorely consumed, there is almost no day on which some new pain or anxiety does not come."*
- *"The wisest servants of God sometimes weaken in the middle of the course, especially when the road is rough and obstructed and the way more painful than expected. How much more, then, should we ask God that he never withdraw the aid of his power among the various conflicts that harass us, but rather that he instill us continually with new strength in proportion to the violence of our conflicts."[43]*

Discouragement is part and parcel of the Christian walk. Everyone will face it at some point—whether you are a giant of the faith or a new believer.

- *Do any of Calvin's statements speak to you or to what you are currently experiencing? If so, which one(s)? Why?*

- *Read Psalm 112 in its entirety. How are the psalmist's words different from Calvin's assessment of his situation?*

• *How could the psalmist have given in to discouragement?*

• *What made the difference in his ability to remain hopeful?*

An Attitude of Thanksgiving

The writer begins Psalm 112 with a shout of celebration and an affirmation of the goodness of God.

- *Reread verses 1–3. How can an attitude of gratitude pull people out of the discouragement they often face in their daily lives?*

- *What should be a believer's response to bad news?*

- *What is your typical response when crises strike? How does this reflect your trust in God's faithfulness—or not?*

- *How can you foster a greater attitude of thankfulness in your daily life?*

An Attitude of Generosity

Another clue to overcome discouragement is found in verses 4–5.

- *According to these verses, what can overcome darkness?*

- *Have you ever been feeling down and discouraged about your own circumstances and then encountered someone who was worse off than you? How did it make you feel?*

- *How might being generous to those in need be an antidote for discouragement?*

- *Who was the last person you were generous to? How did it make you feel?*

 EXPERIENCE GOD'S HEART

Mother Teresa of Calcutta epitomized generosity, particularly during times of discouragement.

> Mother Teresa felt abandoned…In one letter she wrote that she had been walking the streets of Calcutta all day searching for a house where she could start her work.
>
> "At the end of the day, she came back and wrote in her diary, 'Today, I wandered the streets the whole day. My feet are aching and I have not been able to find a home. And I also get the…tempter telling me, "Leave all this, go back to the convent from which you came."'"
>
> She found her home and the rest is history. The Missionaries of Charity feeds 500,000 families a year in Calcutta alone, treats 90,000 leprosy patients annually and educates 20,000 children every year.[44]

Eric Liddell once wrote these words: "Circumstances may appear to wreck our lives and God's plans, but God is not helpless among the ruins. Our broken lives are not lost or useless. God's love is still working. He comes in and takes the calamity and uses it victoriously, working out his wonderful plan of love."[45]

- *What circumstances are trying to wreck your life today?*

• *Has discouragement tried to enter your heart? If so, how can you fend it off?*

• *The next time discouragement tries to pull you down, read the following verses to yourself. If you can read them to yourself in a mirror, even better. Meditate on them and allow them to drop deep into your spirit.*

> Great blessing and wealth fills the house of the wise,
> for their integrity endures forever...
> Life is good for the one who is generous and charitable,
> conducting affairs with honesty and truth.
> Their circumstances will never shake them
> and others will never forget their example.
> They will not live in fear or dread of what may come,
> for their hearts are firm, ever secure in their faith.
> (Psalm 112:3, 5–7)

SHARE GOD'S HEART

Senator Max Cleland, who lost both his legs and his right hand in Vietnam, came to the senators' Bible study withdrawn and tired. One senator said, "Max, are you all right?"

"Not really," he said. "I've been having the same dream for thirty years. I accidentally drop that grenade, and I leap on it, and it explodes and blows my legs off!" That night, the study group gathered around Max and prayed that the Lord would heal the memory.

Two days later, the History Channel broadcasted Max's story. A man from Annapolis saw it and phoned Max: "Senator, you have the story wrong. That wasn't your grenade. It was a young recruit behind you who had opened the pins on his grenades before jumping out of the helicopter. One of them popped out of the belt and rolled on the ground. You leaped on it to save us all. I wrapped you up myself and got you to the hospital. I was on the helicopter; I know how it happened."

Max came to the next Bible study saying a gigantic load had been lifted off his shoulders.

The study group had been studying Romans 8:28, which teaches that God works all things out together for good. After that, when Senator Cleland hurried around in his wheelchair, he would call out to the Senate chaplain, "Remember, things don't work out; God works out things!"[46]

- *How can the perspective of another person concerning what you are facing or feeling change how you think about it?*

- *Who in your life or circle of acquaintances needs encouragement today? How can you help to change their perspective?*

Talking It Out

1. Read Psalm 112:2. How can a life of faith bring blessings to multiple generations? Has this been true in your family? If so, how? If not, how can you start a legacy of blessing with the family you have now?

2. Read the last verse of Psalm 112. Why do you suppose wicked people look at a godly life with an attitude of anger and disdain?

3. Is it a sin to feel discouraged? Why or why not? What does it mean to "encourage yourself in the Lord," and why is it important to a successful Christian walk?

LESSON 11

Comfort When You Need a Purpose

(Psalm 139)

Additional psalm about the need for purpose: 8

Why were you born? Why did God create you and place you on the earth in *this* time, in *this* place, in the family you have, with the friends and job and hobbies and likes and dislikes that you have? In other words, *what is your purpose*?

Nineteen-year-old Cameron Hollopeter was waiting for a train in New York City when he suffered a seizure. His body convulsing out of control, he stumbled down the platform and fell onto one of the tracks—right into the path of an oncoming train.

Fifty-year-old Wesley Autrey was a construction worker who just happened to be standing on the very platform where Cameron had fallen. When he saw the teenager fall onto the tracks, he leaped into action. Grabbing hold of Cameron with only seconds to spare, he rolled with the teenager over into a drainage ditch that was between the two tracks. A mere moment later, the train cars roared over both of them—but because they were in the ditch, neither of them was injured.

Wesley told reporters, "I don't feel like I did something spectacular; I just saw someone who needed help."[47]

Wesley—someone who had the presence of mind to leap into action and the strength to push the teenager out of the way of the train—was in the right place at the right time—for the right purpose.

Likewise:

> Dr. Scott Kurtzman, chief of surgery at Waterbury Hospital, was on his way to deliver an 8 a.m. lecture when he witnessed one of the worst crashes in Connecticut history. The driver of a dump truck had lost control, flipped on its side, and skidded into oncoming traffic. The resulting accident involved twenty vehicles; four people died.
>
> Kurtzman immediately shifted into trauma mode. He worked his way through the mangled mess of people and metal, calling out, "Who needs help?"
>
> After nearly ninety minutes, when all sixteen victims had been triaged and taken to area hospitals, Kurtzman climbed back into his car, drove to the medical school, and began his lecture—two hours late.[48]

The doctor was in the right place at the right time—for the right purpose.

• *What about you? Has there been a time in your life when you knew you were in the right place at the right time— for the right purpose? If so, tell the story.*

- *Or perhaps someone else helped you. They just happened to be at the right place at the right time—for the right purpose. Who was it, and what happened?*

Fearfully and Wonderfully Made

No matter what you are currently experiencing, the Bible has good news: God created you individually. He knows everything about you. He made you, and he loves you. That is the message that David expresses in Psalm 139, one of the most cherished passages of the Bible.

- *Read Psalm 139 in its entirety. What verse(s) stand out to you the most? For what reason?*

- *Write out below your favorite verse from this psalm. What does it mean to you?*

God Knows You

A four-year-old was once trying to learn the Lord's Prayer. He listened carefully to its recitation each Sunday in church until he thought he knew it. Then one Sunday his voice finally rang out, louder than any other: "Our Father who art in heaven, I know You know my name."[49]

God *does* know each of our names! The very first verse of Psalm 139 confirms that there is nothing that the Lord does not know about each of us. Charles Spurgeon once wrote: "The Lord knows us as thoroughly as if he had examined us minutely, and had pried into the most secret corners of our being."[50]

- *How do you feel about God knowing you so intimately?*

- *How do you feel about God knowing you that intimately—and still loving you unconditionally?*

God Is with You Wherever You Are

Do you remember playing hide-and-seek as a child? It was always extra fun to find that super-secret hiding place that no one else could ever find. But what if you hid somewhere that God couldn't find you? We might wish for such a hiding place when we sin just as Adam and Eve tried to hide from the Lord in the garden of Eden after they broke God's command (Genesis 3:1–8). But really, that isn't what we want or need. We need a Savior, one who relentlessly pursues us no matter where we go, one who is with us no matter where the road of life takes us—and that is what we have. God is omnipresent; there is nowhere we can go where he will not be with us.

- *What is the most desolate place you have ever been? Is it difficult for you to picture God in that place? Why or why not?*

- *What does it mean to you that God is with you wherever you go?*

DIGGING DEEPER

God's omnipresence is sometimes misunderstood. It literally means that "God is everywhere present at once." Put negatively, it means that "there is nowhere that God is absent."[51] As David asks, "Where could I go from your Spirit?" (Psalm 139:7). The short answer is nowhere. Or as David says, "It's impossible to disappear from you or to ask the darkness to hide me, for your presence is everywhere" (v. 11). There is no place we can go where God is not.

But *how* is God everywhere present? Over the centuries, Christian theologians have articulated at least three ways that God is present to his creation. One way is by his *knowledge*. God knows everything about everything; he's omniscient. The writer of Hebrews states this truth this way: "There is not one person who can hide their thoughts from God, for nothing that we do remains a secret, and nothing created is concealed, but everything is exposed and defenseless before his eyes, to whom we must render an account" (Hebrews 4:13). God knows everything from the inside out; nothing escapes his gaze.

Another way God is everywhere present is through his *power*. He created the entire universe (Genesis 1; Nehemiah 9:5–6; Hebrews 11:3), he sustains the entire universe in existence moment by moment (Colossians 1:15–17; Hebrews 1:3), and he governs the universe (1 Chronicles 29:11–12). So as Paul told the pagan philosophers in Athens:

> The true God is the Creator of all things. He
> is the owner and Lord of the heavenly realm
> and the earthly realm, and he doesn't live
> in man-made temples. He supplies life and
> breath and all things to every living being…
> He sets the boundaries of people and nations,
> determining their appointed times in history…
> It is through him that we live and function and
> have our identity. (Acts 17:24–26, 28)

Yet a third way God is everywhere present is by his *essence* or *being*. This is perhaps the most difficult aspect of omnipresence to grasp. Theologian Norman Geisler puts it this way:

> What…does omnipresence mean? It means
> that *all of God is everywhere at once*. As the
> indivisible Being, God does not have *one
> part here* and *another part there*, for He has
> no parts. God is *present to* but not *part of*
> creation. God is *everywhere*, but He is not
> *any thing*. He is *at every point in space*, but
> He is not *spatial*. He is *at* every point in
> space, but He is not *of* any point in space.
> There is, of course, a sense in which
> God is "in" the universe but not "of" it: He
> is "in" it (better yet, it is in God) as its Cause
> (Col. 1:16). However, He is not part of the
> *effect*. All of God *is everywhere*, yet *no part
> of God is anywhere*, since He has no parts.[52]

When Solomon completed the temple that his father David had longed to build, he dedicated the structure to God. In his dedication, he offered a prayer, which in part said, "Will God really live on earth among people? Why, even the highest heavens cannot contain you. How much less this Temple I have built!" (2 Chronicles 6:18 NLT). Paul affirmed the same truth when he said in Athens among the temples and shrines that had been built to false gods that the Creator of the universe "doesn't live in man-made temples" (Acts 17:24). Instead, God is everywhere present to all things and sustains all things without existing in all things, like air fills a room or natural gas floods a building. Wherever we go and no matter the circumstances, we can know that God is with us, giving us life and breath, making his resources of comfort and hope available to us, giving us of himself personally and intimately.

God Created You

Not only does God know everything about us, not only does God pursue us wherever we go, not only is he present with us no matter what and where, but he is also the one who knit each of us together in our mother's womb and numbered our days before we were ever born (Psalm 139:13–16).

How intricately was God's involvement when you were in your mother's womb? Consider these words from James Merritt. They provide just a taste of how God made you:

> A single thread of DNA from one human cell contains information equivalent to a library of 1,000 volumes or 600,000 printed pages with 500 words on every page. At conception, one embryo has the equivalent of 50 times the amount of information contained in the Encyclopedia Britannica.[53]

- *What are your favorite physical characteristics about your body? What are your least favorite? What does it mean to know that God designed you with those characteristics?*

- *What about those around you? How does knowing that God designed each person specifically with their physical characteristics help you to view them differently?*

God Has a Purpose for Your Life

> You saw who you created me to be before I
> became me!
> Before I'd ever seen the light of day,
> the number of days you planned for me
> were already recorded in your book. (Psalm
> 139:16)

God had a plan and a purpose for the life of King David. He has a plan and a purpose for you too!

* *Do you know your purpose in this life? If so, what is it?*

* *Solomon wrote, "Let us hear the conclusion of the whole matter: Fear God, and keep his commandments: for this is the whole duty of man" (Ecclesiastes 12:13 KJV). What, then, is the purpose of every believer?*

- How can you better live out this purpose in the next day? The next week? The next year?

🐾 EXPERIENCE GOD'S HEART

Picture in your mind the most valuable works of art in the world. The *Mona Lisa* is actually just a grouping of paintbrush strokes on canvas, probably not worth much in terms of raw materials. What makes this work of art so valuable, worth guarding and protecting with a sophisticated security system, is who its creator was. How much more valuable are you, for you have been carefully and purposefully created by God himself?

- *Are you worth God's guarding and protecting? What do you think?*

• *What has he made you to do? To be?*

• *What do the words in Psalm 139:5 mean to you: "You've gone into my future to prepare the way, and in kindness you follow behind me to spare me from the harm of my past"?*

• *How do you see God working to spare you from what could be the devastating effects of your past?*

- *What do you see him doing to prepare the way for your purpose to be fulfilled?*

- *No one sees the fullness of their own future as God does, and no one understands their past as completely as he does. If you still struggle with your past or your future, trust that God has both well in hand. Thank him for how he can turn your past into something that works for your good, and tell him that you trust him to guide you to a future that will end with you spending forever with him in a new heaven and a new earth and a vast community of fellow believers enjoying the adventure with you (Revelation 21–22).*

SHARE GOD'S HEART

God rarely gives us a purpose that only benefits our own lives. His plans are so much greater than that. His purpose for his children is not only to bless them but also to make them a blessing.

- *In what ways do you see God's purpose for your life bringing blessings to other people?*

- *How can you tap into your purpose this week and share God's love with someone else? If your skill is baking, perhaps make some muffins to share with a neighbor. If you are skilled with writing poetry or comforting words, consider writing a note of encouragement for someone who needs it. Whatever your special skills are—part of the you that God created—use them to glorify him and share his goodness with others.*

Talking It Out

1. Abortion is a "hot" political topic these days. Without creating too much conflict in your group, consider how the words of Psalm 139 inform the abortion debate.

2. God is always with you and knows you completely. Does this idea bother you or bring you comfort as it brought comfort to David? Why?

3. When we think about purpose, we typically consider only what our individual purpose might be. But in light of what Scripture reveals, God also has multiple purposes for every believer's life, such as walking in the power of the Spirit (see Galatians 5:16). Discuss other purposes God has set forth in Scripture for everyone who has embraced Jesus as their Savior and Lord.

LESSON 12

Taking Comfort in God's Promises

(Psalms 105, 126, 132)

Additional psalms about trusting in God's promises: 3, 7, 12

One day C. H. Spurgeon was walking through the English countryside with a friend. As they strolled along, the evangelist noticed a barn with a weather vane on its roof. At the top of the vane were these words: GOD IS LOVE. Spurgeon remarked to his companion that he thought this was a rather inappropriate place for such a message. "Weather vanes are changeable," he said, "but God's love is constant."

"I don't agree with you about those words, Charles," replied his friend. "You misunderstood the meaning. That sign is indicating a truth: Regardless of which way the wind blows, God is love."[54]

No matter which way the wind has been blowing in your life, no matter which type of comfort you may have been seeking from the Lord through the study of the book of Psalms, you can rest on God's promises! No matter what, he loves you, and his care for you is greater than you could ever imagine.

What he has promised you will come to pass. All his words are true. Even if it may seem as if he is distant or has forgotten you in your troubles, he has not—and he never will. Trust him, continue to trust him, and then trust him some more. He has your best interests always at heart, and you can count on him to do what he has said he will do.

Remember What God Has Done

David and the other Old Testament psalmists knew the importance of reciting the promises of God that had been kept already and the promises yet to be fulfilled.

- *Read through Psalm 105. List as many fulfilled promises as you can that were referred to there.*

- *Now do the same with Psalm 126. What fulfilled promises did you find?*

- *Finally, read Psalm 132 and indicate the fulfilled promises below.*

- *Why does rehearsing what God has done in the past help us trust him now and in the future?*

History Is Important

Studying the Bible helps us bring to mind God's history of dealing with his people during those times when we need to renew our faith. But his dealings with people did not stop after the Bible was written.

• *Why is knowing biblical history important?*

• *Why is learning about subsequent church history important?*

- *Why is it important to keep in mind our own personal history in our dealings with the Lord?*

- *In what ways have you made a record of the history of the things God has done for you? If you haven't done so, how might you begin? Consider keeping a faith journal or a scrapbook of promises God has kept in your life. Or brainstorm other ideas. Be as creative as you would like.*

Living Out the Promises

Theologian J. I. Packer writes the following in his book *Knowing God*:

> In the days when the Bible was universally acknowledged in the churches as "God's Word written," it was clearly understood that the promises recorded in Scripture were the proper, God-given basis for all our life of faith, and that the way to strengthen one's faith was to focus it upon particular promises that spoke to one's condition.[55]

- *What did this author believe is the "proper, God-given basis for all our life of faith"?*

- *What did Packer say is the best way to strengthen our faith? How did the writers do this in the psalms we are considering in this lesson?*

- *What promises of God do you need to stand on today?*

 EXPERIENCE GOD'S HEART

> Yes, [God] did mighty miracles and we are
> overjoyed!
> Now, Lord, do it again! Restore us to our former
> glory!
> May streams of your refreshing flow over us
> until our dry hearts are drenched again.
> Those who sow their tears as seeds
> will reap a harvest with joyful shouts of glee.
> They may weep as they go out carrying their
> seed to sow,
> but they will return with joyful laughter and
> shouting with gladness
> as they bring back armloads of blessing and a
> harvest overflowing! (Psalm 126:3–6)

- *What "mighty miracles" are you praying for God to "do again" in your life?*

- *Has the struggle caused weeping or desperation in your heart? Read the promise of the Lord again in Psalm 126:5–6. What will happen for those who "sow their tears as seeds" before God?*

- *What would make you "return with joyful laughter and shouting with gladness" in this situation?*

- *Get real with God. Write a prayer below pouring out your heart to God in your situation, especially if you are renewing your trust in his promises.*

- *How can you faithfully maintain your trust in him, no matter what you face in life?*

 SHARE GOD'S HEART

Charles Spurgeon once said, "God never gives His children a promise which He does not intend them to use."[56] As you have worked your way through this study guide, you have likely encountered many promises of God, many new realizations and truths that brought you comfort in whatever situation you may be facing. Now it is time to put those promises to use—and not just in your life but also in the lives of others.

- *What are some of the lessons you have learned throughout this study of the psalms of comfort?*

- How will these lessons bring changes to your life? To your current situation?

- How can you share these newly realized truths with the people in your life? With your coworkers? With casual acquaintances? Who most needs to hear what you have learned?

Talking It Out

1. How does prayer relate to God's promises being fulfilled in our lives? Do they have an influence on how and what you pray? Why or why not?

2. What role does praise play when we remind ourselves of our past history with the Lord and rehearse his amazing deeds? (Reread Psalm 126 if you need to.) Does praising God change him, or does it change our own hearts? Explain your answer.

3. What did you learn in this study that most stands out to you? How will it make a difference in your walk with God moving forward? What lessons will you commit to living out from now on?

Endnotes

1   Brian Simmons et al., "A Note to Readers," *The Passion Translation: The New Testament with Psalms, Proverbs, and Song of Songs* (Savage, MN: BroadStreet Publishing Group, 2020), ix.

2   James Strong, *Strong's Exhaustive Concordance of the Bible*, Hebrew #4210.

3   Brian Simmons, *The Passion Translation: The New Testament with Psalms, Proverbs, and Song of Songs* (Racine, WI: BroadStreet Publishing, 2015), Psalm 3:2, note 'a.'

4   "The Letter of Athanasius to Marcellinus on the Interpretation of the Psalms," *Theology and Ethics*, accessed November 16, 2022, https://www. theologyethics.com/2016/08/22/the-letter-of-athanasius-to-marcellinus-on-the-interpretation-of-the-psalms/.

5   John Calvin, *John Calvin's Commentaries on the Psalms, Volume 1* (Grand Rapids, MI: Kregel Academic, 2016), 205.

6   Vince Havner, *Playing Marbles with Diamonds and Other Messages for America* (Grand Rapids, MI: Baker Book House, 1985), 94–95, 97.

7   For the dating of Job and his life and the book that bears his name, see Gleason L. Archer Jr., *A Survey of Old Testament Introduction*, rev. ed. (Chicago, IL: Moody Press, 2007), 429–36.

8   D. L. Moody, "Heaven's Inhabitants," Plymouth Brethren Writings, accessed December 1, 2022, https://plymouthbrethren.org/article/1380.

9   Although Abraham prepares to follow God's command to sacrifice his promised son, Isaac, Abraham tells his servants to wait, saying, "The boy and I will travel a little farther. We will worship there, and then *we will come right back*" (Genesis 22:5 NLT, emphasis added). Abraham fully expected that he would return with his son even if that required God to raise his son from death to life at the site of Isaac's sacrifice.

10   For more on what the Old Testament reveals about life after death and even about bodily resurrection, see J. Barton Payne, *The Theology of the Older Testament* (Grand Rapids, MI: Zondervan, 1962), chap. 30; James Orr, "Immortality in the Old Testament," in *Classical Evangelical Essays in Old Testament Interpretation*, ed. Walter C. Kaiser Jr. (Grand Rapids, MI: Baker Book House, 1972), 253–65.

11 Mother Teresa, in Malcolm Muggeridge, *Something Beautiful for God* (New York: Collins, 1972), 73.

12 Bill Gothard, as quoted by David Legge, "The Subject of Loneliness," Preach the Word, 2004, https://www. preachtheword.com/sermon/misc0053-loneliness. shtml.

13 Sociologist and psychologist Sherry Turkle explains this phenomenon and its consequences in her book *Alone Together: Why We Expect More from Technology and Less from Each Other*, rev. ed. (New York: Basic Books, 2017).

14 L. B. Gschwandtner, "The Gallup Survey on Success," Selling Power, Personal Selling Power, Inc., February 2, 2010, https://www.sellingpower. com/2010/02/02/8526/the-gallup-survey-on-success.

15 F. B. Meyer, *Our Daily Walk* (Zeeland, MI: Reformed Church Publications, 2009), 18.

16 Sally Lloyd-Jones, *The Jesus Storybook Bible* (Grand Rapids, MI: ZonderKidz, 2007), 36.

17 Paul Tournier, *The Adventure of Living* (San Francisco, CA: Harper & Row, 1965), 123.

18 See, for example, the excellent discussion by Old Testament scholar Gleason Archer in his book *A Survey of Old Testament Introduction*, 430–34.

19 Psalm 25:5, note 'd,' TPT.

20 John C. Pollock, *A Foreign Devil in China* (Minneapolis, MN: World Wide Publications, 1971), 191, 81.

21 If you would like to study the letter to the Hebrews, see the guide *TPT: The Book of Hebrews: 12-Lesson Bible Study Guide* (Savage, MN: BroadStreet Publishing Group, 2021).

22 See William Palmer, "Roots of Rage," *Chicago Tribune Magazine*, September 28, 1997, https://www.chicagotribune.com/news/ct-xpm-1997-09-28-9709280074-story.html.

23 Paul Miller, *A Praying Life* (Colorado Springs, CO: NavPress, 2017), 125.

24 Kenneth Woodward, "Should You Believe in Miracles?," *Newsweek*, May 1, 2000.

25 Tony Campolo, "Year of Jubilee," Preaching Today, accessed on December 5, 2022, www.preachingtoday.com/sermons/sermons/2005/august/212.html.

26 W. Herschel Ford, *Simple Sermons for Saints and Sinners* (Grand Rapids, MI: Baker, 1954), 9.

27 Psalm 32:2, note 'a,' TPT.

28 Roger Barrier, *Listening to the Voice of God* (Minneapolis, MN: Bethany House, 1998), 55.

29 David Seamonds, *Healing for Damaged Emotions* (Wheaton, IL: Victor Books, 1981), 31–32.

30 Paul Brand and Philip Yancey, "Phantom Pain," *Leadership Journal*, Summer 1984, 55.

31 Psalm 32, note 'b,' TPT.

32 Craig Brian Larson and Phyllis Ten Elshof, eds., *1001 Illustrations That Connect* (Grand Rapids, MI: Zondervan, 2008), 90.

33 A. T. Pierson, *The Hopes of the Gospel* (Manhattan, IL: Fountain of Life Ministries, 2013), 17–19.

34 Adapted from Eva Mozes Kor, *The Twins of Auschwitz* (New York: Monoray, 2020).

35 To learn more about the imprecations in the Psalms,
    see Chalmers Martin, "Imprecations in the Psalms,"
    in *Classical Evangelical Essays in Old Testament
    Interpretation*, 113–32; J. Carl Laney, "A Fresh Look at
    the Imprecatory Psalms," *Bibliotheca Sacra* (January–
    March 1981), 35–45; Derek Kidner, *Psalms 1–72: An
    Introduction and Commentary on Books I and II of
    the Psalms*, Tyndale Old Testament Commentaries,
    ed. D. J. Wiseman (Downers Grove, IL: InterVarsity
    Press, 1973), 25–32; A. F. Kirkpatrick, *The Book of
    Psalms*, reprint ed. (Grand Rapids, MI: Baker Book
    House, 1906), lxxxviii–xciii; Robert B. Chisholm Jr., "A
    Theology of the Psalms," in *A Biblical Theology of the
    Old Testament*, ed. Roy B. Zuck (Chicago: Moody Press,
    1991), 281–84; Walter C. Kaiser Jr., *Hard Sayings of
    the Old Testament* (Downers Grove, IL: InterVaristy
    Press, 1988), chap. 48.

36 Norman L. Geisler, *Systematic Theology, Volume Two*
    (Minneapolis, MN: Bethany House, 2003), 323.

37 Adapted from Wilbur Konkel, *Living Hymn Stories*
    (Minneapolis, MN: Bethany Fellowship, 1971), 69–73.

38 A. W. Tozer, *The Knowledge of the Holy* (New York:
    Harper & Row, 1961), 57.

39 Tozer, *The Knowledge of the Holy*, 59–60.

40 Lee Strobel, *The Case for Faith* (Grand Rapids, MI:
    Zondervan, 2000), 96.

41 Glenn Wasson, "A Wing and a Prayer," *Reader's Digest*, March 1997.

42 Legge, "The Subject of Loneliness."

43 William J. Bouwsma, *John Calvin: A Sixteenth-Century Portrait* (New York: Oxford University Press, 1988), 26–27.

44 Satinder Bindra, "Archbishop: Mother Teresa Underwent Exorcism," CNN, September 7, 2001, https://edition.cnn.com/2001/WORLD/asiapcf/ south/09/04/mother.theresa.exorcism/.

45 Eric Liddell, *The Disciplines of the Christian Life* (New York: Ballantine Books, 1988), 115.

46 Larson and Ten Elshof, eds., *1001 Illustrations That Connect*, 199.

47 Cara Buckley, "Man Is Rescued by Stranger on Subway Tracks," *The New York Times*, January 3, 2007, https://www.nytimes.com/2007/01/03/ nyregion/03life.html.

48 Larson and Ten Elshof, eds., *1001 Illustrations That Connect*, 178.

49 See Larson and Ten Elshof, eds., *1001 Illustrations That Connect*, 107.

50   Charles Spurgeon, *Treasury of David: Psalms 111–150, Vol. 3b* (Grand Rapids, MI: Zondervan, 1979), 258.

51   Geisler, *Systematic Theology, Volume Two*, 169.

52   Geisler, *Systematic Theology, Volume Two*, 170, italics in the original.

53   James Merritt, "The Mystery of Creation," Touching Lives, August 9, 2021, https://www.touchinglives.org/devotionals/the-mystery-of-creation.

54   "C. H. Spurgeon," Bible.org, February 2, 2009, https://bible.org/illustration/c-h-spurgeon-0.

55   J. I. Packer, *Knowing God* (Downer's Grove, IL: InterVarsity Press, 1973), 103.

56   Charles Spurgeon, *Spurgeon's Sermons, Volume 2* (Carol Stream, IL: Hendrickson, 2011), 404.

MY THOUGHTS

MY THOUGHTS

MY THOUGHTS

MY THOUGHTS